NATURAL
HOME SCHOOLING
A Parent-Teacher's Guidebook
To Natural Learning In The Home

About the Author

Kerri Bennett Williamson is a free-lance writer, artist, designer, and instructor who has been involved in the home schooling movement since 1984. She has been continuing her education, learning naturally, since graduating from high school. Although pursuing a degree has not yet become a priority for Kerri, those who know her best consider her to be well educated in many areas of study.

Kerri and her husband are parents of four children (aged seven, nine, eleven and eighteen) and have been home schooling for eleven years. She served as newsletter coordinator and editor (three years), and a director (one year) for H.A.N.A. (Homeschooler's Association of Northern Alberta). Kerri continues to share her home schooling experiences and knowledge through personal conversations and public seminars.

NATURAL
HOME SCHOOLING

A Parent-Teacher's Guidebook
To Natural Learning In The Home

By

KERRI BENNETT WILLIAMSON

CHARLES C THOMAS • PUBLISHER
Springfield • Illinois • U.S.A.

Published and Distributed Throughout the World by

CHARLES C THOMAS • PUBLISHER
2600 South First Street
Springfield, Illinois 62794-9265

© *1995 by* CHARLES C THOMAS • PUBLISHER

ISBN 0-398-05977-2 (cloth)
ISBN 0-398-05978-0 (paper)

Library of Congress Catalog Card Number: 94-46770

With THOMAS BOOKS *careful attention is given to all details of manufacturing
and design. It is the Publisher's desire to present books that are satisfactory as to
their physical qualities and artistic possibilities and appropriate for their particular
use.* THOMAS BOOKS *will be true to those laws of quality that assure a good
name and good will.*

Printed in the United States of America
SC-R-3

Library of Congress Cataloging-in-Publication Data

Williamson, Kerri Bennett.
    Natural home schooling : a parent-teacher's guidebook to natural
learning in the home / by Kerri Bennett Williamson.
        p.   cm.
    Includes bibliographical references (p.   ).
    ISBN 0-398-05977-2. — ISBN 0-398-05978-0 (pbk.)
    1. Home schooling—United States.   2. Education—Parent
participation—United States.   3. Public schools—United States.
I. Title.
LC40.W56   1995
649'.68—dc20   94-46770
                                                                              CIP

To Natural Home Schooling:
the protecting and nurturing of a child's mind, body and spirit
within the natural family unit, rather than without.

To The Natural Family Unit:
the natural institution where at least one child is protected and nurtured by
at least one or ideally both male and female parents (natural or adopted).

INTRODUCTION

In the five years since my book: *HOME SCHOOLING: Answering Questions* was published, I have continued to share what I have been learning about home schooling with those in my community through private conversations and public seminars. Increasingly, more people have become interested and open to the idea of keeping children home to school while the home schooling movement has continued to expand, year by year, becoming relatively common in some areas.

The rising tide of private and home schools can be attributed to the broad societal dissatisfaction with numerous facets of the public school phenomenon in general and possibly diverse religious, political and ideological views in particular. Success of private and home schools is in direct proportion to failure of public schools.

While those who pursue the possibility of home schooling their children can find solutions with legalities, they are often at a loss when it comes to curriculum and confidence in their own home school. Help is available to them, particularly structured home schooling curriculums, usually at some cost; but when parents choose the natural path of holistic learning, they often feel afloat on a small raft at sea.

It is for those parents that I have written this sequel to my first book about home schooling. In an effort not to repeat myself in this work, there may be information you missed from the previous one. I hope this book can stand on its own, but if it seems a little shaky in spots, and you feel left with questions, you may find the answers in *HOME SCHOOLING: Answering Questions.*

Back to introducing this book. As a home schooling mother of four, having been free from the unnaturalness of the public schools for over ten years, I am happy to share my thoughts on letting children learn naturally, as I believe they were meant to.

The more I watch my children grow and learn, as I gently guide, nurture, provide for and protect them, the more I believe in home schooling, naturally. It's the natural alternative to public schooling. It's the winning choice as opposed to the losing battle the public schools are waging.

What the public schools are waging is more than a battle for brains; it has become a war against souls and society, in the social reforming public schooling officials' efforts to socialize children into pliable and compliable state subjects. Good old, time-tested morals have been exchanged for contrived, politically correct ideals and school imposed values clarification that often undermines home values.

As the public schools lose the battle for better brains, they are winning the war on the minds of North America's children and all to the tune of increasing tax dollars. What the public school does to its children, parents pay for, whether they want it or not. If parents were to find out what their children were actually learning, they might look for alternatives. Private schools do far better at brain building at half the price and home schools are the ideal natural choice, from parents at no charge, with love and a library card.

If you could only see what I see; if you could hear what I hear; or feel what I feel; then you would know what I will try to tell you. Perhaps I can convey what I have learned about children and learning through these years.

You would understand that children don't need to go blocks or miles away to a big brick building with barred windows to be able to learn what they need to know to grow up and make a living and live a good life. Institutional school is not the only way. Public school is the common way to be sure, but to help children above the common, there are better ways. Home schooling is a natural.

CONTENTS

NATURAL
HOME SCHOOLING
A Parent-Teacher's Guidebook
To Natural Learning In The Home

PUBLIC SCHOOLING, UNNATURALLY

1. SOUNDS

The still morning air cringes as a piercing buzz rings out through our neighborhood. In the distance grows a noise: a humming, screaming, yelling, tangibly audible thing. It's recess time again. While the school is blocks away, perhaps a mile or two, the noise always seems to reach us.

We've always preferred to live away from the schools, but, eventually, you run into another one. Public schools are everywhere. We love the playgrounds and the park areas, minus the frequently common garbage, foul language (scrawled and spoken) and broken glass, but the noise can spoil a quiet neighborhood.

I can see them now, bursting out of the school doors: children of every size, shape and color, running for the swings, slides, monkey bars and space. I can hear them: screams in competition with other screams. Scream above scream above scream, like hands climbing up a bat to see who gets on top, who's first, who wins. Who is noticed. Who is heard.

One day as we passed a school playground, at recess time, my eldest daughter (who was four or five at the time) asked me why the children were screaming like that. She was very concerned. She thought something was very wrong, that the children were extremely upset to be screaming like that. I had to ponder on the inquiry somewhat. I hadn't really stopped to wonder why school kids scream so much at recess.

In searching for an answer for my daughter, a thought dawned on me: in the classroom, children must sit with their mouths shut. The teacher does the talking and the kids are supposed to listen.

I found myself explaining to my children that kids in school must hold in all their talking for about ninety minutes and so that must be why they explode in screams and yelling at recess, noon, recess and after school again.

There were many days after that one, many recesses, when I listened to the screaming school children a mile or more away, and I thought. I felt for those children, so full of energy, so chattery, with so much to say, so much to ask; how they had to hold it all in, ninety minutes at a time, and then only fifteen minutes to release it. Scream against scream, noise to noise, no one really listening to them: no one wanting to listen to all that noise.

As I watched my children chatter softly through the days, I began to appreciate how difficult it must be for children to learn to master verbal skills of our language when their lips are zipped so much each day. Kids need to talk, to practice speech in order to master the skill. But, it's the teacher who talks. And the children must listen. And listen and listen-... and then they get to scream for fifteen, before they listen and listen again.

The unnatural silence imposed upon the mouths of babes is just the beginning of the unnaturalness of the public school. Every year that we continue to home school our children, I see more clearly how public school is an unnatural institution manufactured by political planners and social reformers. Public schools are made more for the convenience of society than for the educational edification of society's children. Public schools are for parents who want a socially acceptable free child-watch system rather than a place for children to learn.

One of the many things children do learn at school can be heard in the school yards and in back alleys and in malls: those assorted four-letter words that so many children know how to spell, no matter how illiterate they remain. The sounds of street talkers are heard, ringing out throughout most neighborhoods in North America. These are the sounds of the public school. Screaming and swearing are sounds perpetuated by them. It's only unnatural.

2. METHODS

There are teachers and then there are teachers. Teaching, the word: to impart knowledge or skill; give instruction. Teaching, the profession: certified and uncertified teachers, instructors and professors. Teachers; the school marms and school masters.

The typical public school teacher has gone to a university to achieve a bachelor's degree in education, having studied general subjects, having student taught and then secured a job as a teacher.

The teaching methods and courses of study change over the years. New methods are brought in to improve upon the old ones and then old ones are brought back because new ones don't work. The public school teaching methods come and go as the public schools try to find methods that work.

This public school system of teacher-learning is a continual trial and error process that uses the publicly schooled kids as little guinea pigs in a lab. The public schools don't know what works. They try to figure out what works by testing the kids to try to find out if and what the kids have learned. When the methods fail to teach the kids, the kids fail.

So kids are failing in the schools because the schools are failing to teach the kids. The schools just keep on flailing and failing, flailing about, trying this method and that one, recycling old ones, calling them new ones, fooling the parents and students alike, failing families while the students are failing school.

The public school system gives children a relatively few selected answers while it doesn't even answer their unending questions. In the words of Neil Postman, "Children enter school as question marks and leave as periods."

Margaret Meade explained, "My grandmother wanted me to have an education, so she kept me out of school." I applaud her grandmother. Public schools' teaching methods don't ensure a proper, satisfactory or, more especially, an excellent education, just a common one.

From rote memorization to self-directed learning, from testing to evaluating, from the back-to-basics lessons to twenty-first century curriculums, public schools have tried them all. Educational experts across the continent or city centers cannot agree on which methods work and neither can the parents, particularly in larger schools in bigger cities where varying belief systems conflict.

If public schools saw parents as customers like successful private schools do, methods would at least be chosen in response to the customers' requests and to their satisfaction. The public school is just another long arm of the state, where the children are little appendages and the parents are cut off from the system.

Many enlightened educators and clear thinking parents have been demanding an educational voucher system for years. This system has worked in the few areas it has been tried, and would work across the continent if it were applied, because parents would tend to choose the methods and schools that work. The biggest reasons the voucher system has not been implemented beyond a couple of pilot projects are quite simply because public schools would stand nearly empty and public school teachers would strike out.

The voucher system is full of choices. The political and educational elite do not want to give parents the choices they desire for their children. Most parents would like to choose the teaching methods they believe in. In the public schooling system, this is almost impossible.

A parent is more likely to recognize what methods of teaching or learning would work with their own children, but this knowledge remains irrelevant as long as their children remain in a public school. The only way a parent can act on this knowledge is by carefully choosing a private school or by forming their own home school. The school chooses the methods.

3. BOREDOM

If the children are listening, does it really mean they are learning? I can see the little children and not so little kids sitting in their desks now. Little heads nodding, sleepily, some trying to stay upright, trying to learn; others just trying to get away with a few Z's without getting caught. Eyes blinking, closing, wandering, meandering, looking for something interesting to latch onto. Mouths itching to chatter or nibble or yawn.

Stomachs growling, legs twitching, arms wiggling, bodies squirming. Little, middle-sized and big kids locked into their wooden desks when they would rather be relaxing or recreating somewhere else. Anywhere but here. Bodies, minds and souls focused on one thing: the end of the school day and then the school week and then the year end.

It is no small wonder that kids look forward to the summer holidays, when school's out for summer. It isn't long into the school year before children are bored of school and each holiday becomes time off to look forward to. Each holiday becomes a break from the boredom.

While some children can and do get bored as the summer might drag on for them, I suggest that it is more like a school withdrawal symptom. Public schooling teaches children to sit and listen as passive learners, if they are really learning in the truest sense of the word. Children are in the habit of public schooling and the habit might be a little hard to break. Bad habits are like that.

Children are born to learn and they learn to walk and talk in a natural way, step by step, word by word, sentence by sentence. When they walk into the public school, their talking slows as they are told to listen, their walking halts as they are told to sit, and their learning retards as they are spoon-fed bits and pieces of the public school curriculum.

The natural and spontaneous love of learning and zest for life is squashed by the public school. Creativity and self-motivation is smothered. The public school negates so much of what the child has learned about how to learn by their fifth or sixth birthday. Some children remember how to learn on their own on weekends and holidays and especially in the summer. Some have more difficulty recalling such self-directed learning.

When children look forward to school near the end of summer, they look forward to making new friends or having something to do or perhaps they are just looking forward to some adult attention. Maybe these children aren't getting the family time that is really what they seek. Family stability and time with family has become far too rare.

The public school has been a major thrust in chipping away at the family stability that was the cornerstone of a more stable society we once knew. The phenomenon of the unnatural public school perpetuates the societal ball rolling down the hill, taking the family with it.

When children break the public schooling habit by home schooling and after their withdrawal symptoms subside, they can get down to real learning. When children are set free from the public school habit and rehabilitated away from the addiction the schooling system imposes, they get a chance to live without the boredom so common in the public schools.

Bored to sleep, bored silly, bored sick, bored to tears, bored to death. Death of a school child. Death of curiosity. Death of the spirit. Death of learning.

4. FORGOTTEN

Piece upon piece of information pressed into tiny little brains, squeezed in to make them grow bigger and bigger until that final day when they have arrived into adulthood, learned individuals. Is that how children learn?

John Holt once said that the only difference between bright children and slow children is that bright children remember what they've been taught long enough to take and pass the tests. Everybody forgets what they've been taught, the slow children just forget a little sooner.

Many of us did well in school, but how many of us can remember what we learned in the past as time passes? The first weeks back at school in September are spent reviewing what was taught and supposed to be learned the year before.

"Education is what survives when what has been learned has been forgotten," as W. H. Auden has said, and unfortunately, much of what is covered in public schools is forgotten all too soon. I did well in school. I even did well in math. Don't ask me to take any math-related tests now. I can't remember a thing. I memorized the formulas and passed the tests back then, but within a very short time after leaving school, I'd forgotten everything I didn't care about. I didn't care about math. I didn't care about a lot of things I memorized. I was there to get the marks and get out. That was life at that time.

Rather than teaching kids to memorize countless facts that they will soon forget, it makes more sense to teach kids how to find facts when they need them. Albert Einstein did not even memorize his own phone number and when asked why, he answered that he didn't want to clutter his mind with information that he could easily look up.

To be honest, I tried to remember everything I memorized. It's just that it's not that easy to remember things you're required to remember. What we are required to remember is far more likely to fall into that territory of forgotten lessons than those things we learn having been curious to know about them.

As a child, I remember asking my parents and teachers why I had to memorize or learn something that I was going to forget later anyway. They explained to me that I had to prove I could learn something by passing the tests. When I asked why I had to learn something I'd likely never need or use, if I did happen to remember it, they said that I needed to exercise my brain. Practice learning, stretch your brain, expand the space between the ears.

Does the exercise of memorizing required information expand the learning powers? Certainly not like real learning does. Curiosity is a naturally instinctive power that drives children toward answers to their questions. Finding answers to questions is one prime facet of what real learning is. Memorization of meaningless facts is a manmade and unnatural chore.

If a child learns enough of what is taught in school to pass the tests, that learning isn't all going to last forever. Only the information which was interesting and important to the child will be remembered to any degree by that child. Public schools produce forgotten lessons.

5. WRONGS

"What did you learn at school today, honey?" I asked my publicly schooled son.

He answered, "Nuthin."

"Why do you always say nothing, when I ask you what you learned in school?"

Another thought-provoking answer, "I dunno."

"When are you going to say something besides I don't know and nothing?"

First a pause and then exasperation, "Mom!?" He didn't know what else to say. That's all he had to say about school. If I pressed him a little, sat down with him, spent a little time with him, I might find out a thing or two that they did at school.

Almost invariably, the conversation would get to the playground. It seemed like most of the memories were made there, as if the whole waking day had been spent there. Recess seemed to be school life.

As my son spoke of recess and the playground, I learned what he was learning at school. Some of the information took years to come out. My son was out of the public schools for two years before I finally learned everything he had really been learning at school, during recess, in the playground.

He learned about listening outwardly while ignoring inwardly. He learned to block out the noise, the world and the pains of it. He learned about joining forces with allies (some classmates) to go against enemies (everybody else). He learned how to tease and to ridicule. He learned and heard how to speak coarse language and about being cool with cigarettes and the fun of innocent rope-burns around necks. My son learned all about antisocial behavior at public schools. He learned how to compromise our beliefs and to bend to the brainwashings of fellow students (and teachers, too).

He was taught about gonchee pulls and groin grabs (the squeeze the balls routine) for guys and panty pulls for girls who were grabbed and depanted by groups of guys (and horrifyingly, sometimes girls were fingered). He learned about humping (mock rape), pornography and masturbation. And then there were threats of injury by jackknives and switchblades. And all this by the end of the second grade, in three different good schools in nice, upper-middle class neighborhoods of a tame town where violence is rare by comparison.

This doesn't even address the gangs, guns, rampant rape and violence that grows like a plague across North America. For whatever reasons, these horrors are sweeping through the public schools. Good families should be free from such evils. It is wrong to expect good parents to send their children to schools that harbor and even foster such atrocities.

There are many who like to blame all the violence on poverty. We need only to look back to a time when the poor in America were poorer than the poor today, and poverty was not a license for violence and violence was not excused by poverty. Poverty is no excuse for violence against innocent victims. Two wrongs don't make a right, right? Just more wrongs.

Speaking of more wrongs and then of poverty, North America's debts spell poverty (read between the lines), and some of this poverty is caused by public schooling costs. The more I have learned about the costs of education, the more I am amazed at the dollar figures and what they buy. The average public school in North America spends at least $6000 per child per year with poor results, while the average private school spends less than $3000 per child per year with rich results.

Why does a public school cost more for less? Forget about the teacher to student ratio. Perhaps one cause is the official to student ratio in the public school. In private schools, the administrator to student ratio is very low while in the public schools, the administrator to student ratio is many times higher. There is an excessive amount of administrators in the public schools. Bureaucracy abounds.

Studies show that the more a school spends per student, the worse the students seem to do. The more a public school spends, the worse the students do. Perhaps this is like spoiled little rich kids who get everything they want except for love (and then there are the public school people using money to perpetuate themselves—more money, more power). Those private schools that survive on meager budgets produce students who thrive (they have to stick to the basics because that is all they can afford). The lower the dollar figures, the higher the scores. That seems to be the rule rather than the exception. Many home schooling kids are excelling on a zero budget which includes only a library card. When kids are free to learn, they can learn for free.

Taxpayers need not spend anything to educate the nation's children. Free people should be free to teach their own children. Children can and do learn for free. How much has been spent to teach millions upon millions of children how to walk and talk? Socialists want the schooling of students of the state. Socialists want to promote socialism and there is no better way than to start with the young. Socialists cry for universal daycare so they can start from the womb.

A free country can't afford socialism. Taxpayers can't afford to foot the bills for programs they don't want or need and in fact are harmful to freedom. Our great grand children will be paying for the big bills of a bad school deal most of us don't want or need. Who needs bad medicine? Why should we pay for it?

All this just echoes the same state of affairs of the state at large. Public or government organizations almost always cost twice as much as private corporations to do half as well at best. That's another can of worms that belongs in another book.

Back to more wrongs. With no-fault morality being taught in the public schools under such names as Moral Values Education and Values Clarification, kids are learning that there is no right or wrong, just justification for unjust conduct. As if kids can't come up with enough excuses for bad behavior and self-justification for wrong-doing, teachers have been teaching them more. There is no evil, there is no wrong, just reaction to unfairness, they say.

Beyond denigrated values, kids in public schools are also taught counter-cultural beliefs that go against their family ideals, more often than not. While the average parent believes in the freedom ideals that North America was founded and built upon, the average public school teacher presses communism (under numerous other softened names and pleasant sounding titles that truly mean communism or at least socialism which leads to the same in the end) into the pliable minds of the young. Communism and socialism have been substituted for true democracy in school textbooks all across North America, and the reformers are rewriting history: from Christopher Columbus to the founding fathers and more.

The expensive textbooks that fill the public schools' library shelves and desk drawers *are* being systematically emptied of all *politically incorrect* information and replaced with the *politically correct*, in keeping with social reformers' theoretical communally utopic ideals. *He* is being replaced with *she* (especially in examples of power, influence or traditionally male professions . . . but never as rapist, murderer, criminal or evil doer), *traditional families* (dad, mom and child/ren) are being replaced by *any grouping of individuals residing together,* and so on.

Between the no-fault morals that kids are taught to practice without guilt and the ideals teachers preach with religious fervor, the gap between parents and their children grows ever wider. There have been times when I thought that the generation gap was a public school accidental evolution downward, but it becomes ever clearer that there have been armies of socialists since before the dawn of communism, intent on winning their war against freedom. They won Eastern Europe and some of Asia through force and they are winning much of the rest of the world through subterfuge.

Many leaders and proponents of communism and other socialisms, know the power of the public school to bring about the changes they seek. From Plato to Marx and on down the communalism trail, they all preach public schools as the means to mold the minds of the young to their own ends. Their ultimate end is communism. Communism is the end of community.

Some would argue that nationwide family breakdown is the cause of all these woes and the public school is where these problems can be solved. I contend that the public school is very probably one of the major factors causing the breakdown of the family and it's time to reclaim the family.

While it may be true that public schools offer abused and neglected kids something better than they get at home (I would hate to see how bad those homes are), kids from good homes fare far better at home where life is right (for the most part and even in flawed families) as opposed to the schools where so much is wrong. Troubled kids from troubled homes bring their troubles to school. Troubles abound at the public schools and the wrongs grow like a bad weed.

6. RIGHTS

If you do a crime, you'll do the time. Commit a wrong, lose your rights. Most of us won't argue that when guilty criminals lose some rights because of their wrongs, it's rightly so. Just and justified. Unfortunately for society, criminals often get off too soon or too easily, but that's another story. Many of us would argue with the softened state.

Why don't we argue about the lost rights of the innocent? Why do children, the most innocent of all of us, lose so many rights that they would fight for if they knew they could win? Why don't we even think for a second that children have the right to be free from being locked up in an institution?

The bad guys go to jail and have much of their freedoms impounded until they have paid in time for their crime—crimes like theft, vandalism, assault, assorted violence, arson, rape and murder. These evil doers are pulled out of society to protect society and to punish the committer of the crime.

What are society's benefits from penning up children? Why are children's rights not even considered in the schooling picture? Children are punished and told it is for their own good. They are forced into institutions against their wills in the guise of giving them an equal chance at an education.

Many children like school and want to go, some of the time. But, even children who are popular with peers and pets of teachers want to stay home from school sometimes. Charles Shultz said it well through Charlie Brown: "Happiness is . . . being sick enough to stay home from school, but not too sick to watch TV."

Some educational reformers suggest a voluntary schooling system. Kids could go to school when, where and with whom they want. Bad teachers and bad schools would be avoided. Kids would go because they want to. There would be less rebellion and more cooperation. Most people can't handle the thought of giving kids that much choice. Too much freedom, too many rights.

While I believe children must be guided and guarded by their parents, and I know they cannot be given the rights of adults, if only because they cannot accept the responsibilities of adults, I also believe that children are born with rights that they are not given. The freedoms many little children enjoy for five years (except for daycare tots) are suddenly removed for thirteen long years when kindergarten rears its counterfeit head (copying the fun free home environment, hiding the real world of school brought on by the first grade).

Public school denies children the rights they deserve and steals the rights they've owned since birth. Many parents want their children cared for in the public school system. Why call it school in that case? We should call it a child watch system. When its prime function is to free-up parents from their parental responsibilities during weekdays, it's more baby-sitter than teacher.

Mandatory state schooling is a type of mass state kidnapping of children. When the state school imposes its ideals (to the tune the special interest groups demand we all sing) upon children it has forcibly taken into custody, we should give it another name: the longest thought-reform arm of the state.

The formative years are precious ones and public schools take these years from the parents and their children to teach children more than just the three R's. Proper socialization is a prime focus. The schools take it upon themselves to teach the children to become good citizens of the state.

When I think of what goes on in the schools, brainwashing comes to mind. I think some of it is. Brainwashing: a method for systematically changing attitudes or altering beliefs . . . any method of controlled systematic indoctrination . . . , as *Webster's Dictionary* describes, connotes some of what the public schools are doing, well intentioned or not.

Severing children's rights so completely is completely wrong. All the reasons glare in the face of the innocent child who wants to stay and play at home, "Why do I have to leave and go to school to read and count, Mommi? I can read and count here at home. Why do I have to find friends at school? I have friends here near home."

Any kid with a library card can learn more than is learned in the public schools. Even TV can teach kids more than what they learn at school (learning channels offer marvelous history, math, science and nature programs and beyond). Computers offer even more learning opportunities—many of which are interactive. Add a modem and a kid can connect to others around the world from a phone line and through computer bulletin board services (BBS's), many of which are free, asking for optional minimal donations or small fees. With the advanced technologies of today, and the prices plummeting while the products soar (easier to use while they become less costly and more amazing), a child need not ever leave home to expand his or her mind.

The public school boards and their officials will never let the public know how well thousands of home schooling kids have done, even excelling, especially when compared to the public school product. This is one schooling success story that they won't share, because it would be bad press for them. The public school can't afford to let the masses know that all a kid needs for schooling success is a little love and a library card. This is left up to a few tabloids ("Truant Goat Farmer Boys Get Scholarships to Harvard" for example, speaking of the home schooling Colfax brothers), and thankfully, some magazines and books where the occasional home schooling success story is published. The public school will never publish information that will be so damning to them.

Now that home schoolers are again proving that kids don't have to go to schooling institutions to learn and even excel, only kids who want or need to go to school should go. Only parents who want or need a child care service should use the schools. Those of us who want to keep our children at home sweet home, should. Home schooling gives children their rights.

7. PEER DEPENDENCE

Quantitative same-aged peer association shouldn't be confused with quality associations. While kids do and should want friends of their age, they should be able to choose their friends. In the public school, children are forced into unpleasant peer associations like nowhere else.

Of all the opportunity for friends that seem available to kids at public schools, there are in reality very few. While in school, kids might think they have many friends. It is true they have many associations, but friends are a far different people than acquaintances.

Making an acquaintance might be the beginning of a friendship, but a friendship it does not make. Public school is full of associations, acquaintanceships and the like; but true friends are hard to come by. Superficial friends come easy, but true friendships must be worked hard for. It takes some of us many years to figure this out.

Time meant by nature to be spent with family is spent with groups of same-aged peers. The family institution, as it was meant to be, disintegrates in the manmade institution: the public school. Caught in the superficial world of school, kids think they have loyal friends where they have superficial ones and give their loyalties to the undevoted. Bonds to the family broken, the peer bonds begin and the generation gap widens. The public school begat the generation gap and peer-dependence.

Peer-dependence is a sad or pitifully funny thing at best and a dangerous and sometimes deadly one at worst. Peer-dependence spurs kids to tease, to bully, to steal, to vandalize, to assault, and even to rape and murder. Peer-dependence gives birth to groupies and gangs, bimbos and criminals. While a bad home may be the birth of origin, peer-dependence can solidify and propel the bad to worse; and persuade kids from good homes to go bad.

Gangs aren't a new phenomenon. There were gangs when I was young. There were gangs when my parents were young. There were gangs when my grandparents were young. Gangs do seem to be a phenomenon of cities and schools, though. Whenever and wherever children roam and coagulate in groups, gangs form. Some gangs are harmless, more or less. Other gangs are deadly. Remember *The Lord of the Flies?* Think about Los Angeles where thousands die each year in the midst of gang warfare. Think about the gang violence in other big cities.

Your children need not be victims of gang gunshots to be injured.

There are varying degrees of harm that gang mentality inflicts on innocent children who are often just bystanders. Sticks and stones break teeth and bones, but names hurt too. When I was serving time in a public school in my early years, there grew a girls' gang there. I refused to join them, simply because I could see that they had nothing better to do than to harass and hurt (physically and mentally) whomever they chose as victim of the week. Each week, the chosen victim would come to my side and I would come to her defense. It was a rotating door and I stood alone on the outside. The week I was chosen, I was completely alone.

Another lesson in human nature; it reminds me of the bell curve. I think of a few shepherds at the top, multiples of sheep in the middle and a few wolves at the bottom. Strong-willed people can gravitate towards bad or good, and weak-willed people gravitate to either side. The strong who lean towards good will lead some weak to the good while the strong who lean towards bad will lead some weak to the bad. Leaders and followers. Good and bad. A simplistic view, but it's generally true.

I've seen far too many children hurt by gang activities and gang mentality. Gangs can hurt kids, whether kids join them or not. It doesn't matter whether kids are in or out of a gang, they can be harmed by association within or hurt by persecution without.

Most parents don't hang around the playgrounds, the schools, the parks and the malls long enough to see and comprehend how much gang mentality abounds and how much harm is doled out to children and teens because of them.

Gang association is not a natural thing. Families are. Children are not born into gangs. They join them when they feel estranged from their families. Children are born into families. That is nature's way. Parents and children. Gangs are a product of neglect. Kids need families for the supervision and association that prevents gang cohesion.

The more time children spend with their family, the more likely they will form positive bonds with their parents and siblings. This positive bonding is a foundation for successful relationships throughout life. The more time children spend running around with other children, the more likely they will form the negative bonds that gangs are. This negative bonding germinates relationship failures.

While peer-dependence is a teen-hood thing most of us grow out of when we finally grow up, some never really recover from it and many of us are left with scars. There is certainly damage done to families and some things lost are never again found.

8. HIERARCHY

From hierarchy to monarchy to anarchy, the school seems to have it all. From social class and caste systems to power tripping and kingdom building to chaos and confusion, democracy and natural order seem dead while bureaucracy and plenty of red tape thrive, alive and well in the public school.

Hierarchy is: "any system of persons or things ranked one above the other; the power or dominion of a hierarch"; *Webster's Dictionary* tells us. From the testing and grading systems to the age separate classes and authority of teachers and principles, the public schools definitely have a hierarchical system.

Public schools seem to prepare kids to accept life in the hierarchical lane while the schooling officials preach individuality, a sense of self and other such lofty ideals that nature giveth freely and the school hath taken away.

Within the structure of the school board and on down through principles and to teachers and then those kids who seem to lead amongst the masses of school students, there is a type of monarchy. Through *Webster's*, we find meaning to the word monarchy: "a sole and absolute ruler of a state; one who or that which holds a dominant position."

Dominance predominates. The meekest and lowliest children submit to their more powerful peers, who then bow down to teachers, who bend to principles, who are ruled by superintendents and so on.

And then there are those teens who wreak havoc, rebelling against rules and those teachers who manipulate and even molest. Insanity reigns and anarchy rules. *Webster's* shows Anarchy: "social disorder due to absence of . . . control; confusion, chaos, disorder."

Public school's attempt at bringing about social order has succeeded in destroying much of nature's order, and supplanted in nature's place a socialized controlling system that fails to control. Public schools don't give society what they promise. Full of contradictions and unnaturalness, public school would have failed, except that it has and holds public funds. Survival of the fittest does not apply here. Public schools survive to this day because they are the fattest: full of the public purse.

Public funds are the power of the public school. Money gives it it's strength. When the public school shows signs of further failures, it cries out for more money as the solution. Like a king and queen in an ivory tower, demanding more and more taxes of their people to keep pace with their ever increasing expensive tastes, public schooling officials are out of touch with the children they profess to teach and the parents they are supposed to serve.

It doesn't seem to matter how much money the public school consumes; it doesn't seem to improve itself. In fact, it worsens. Blame is cast at the doors of the family home. Parents are scolded. Children are failed. Poverty is incriminated in the crime of illiteracy. Taxpayers are scolded for not wanting to share more money for the children. Everyone but the public school officials and teachers themselves are blamed for the failures and problems of the public school. Everyone, meaning children and their parents.

Public school failed to go public a long time ago, perhaps at its inception. The public only has a share in the costs and consequences of the public school. People do not share in the curriculum planning. Parents are not allowed to share in the decision-making process. The public school is a Kingdom that has failed its people and the people need to begin the dismantling of it before it dismantles them as a people.

Maybe we the people need to begin a great revolution. Begin with a revolt against the school by saving your children from it. Enroll in a private school or better still, your own home school. Revolt against taxes in one way or another. Demand school or educational vouchers at least, so that parents can vote for the schooling of their choice with their vouchers. The best schools will win. Public schools will become privatized, reformed to the public's satisfaction, or die. Down with the Public School Kingdom! Up with schools of the people! Schools of the people, by the people, for the people.

9. PSEUDOFAMILY

The principle-father, the teacher-mother and the classmate-siblings. The class-family pictures. The classroom-living room. The playground-backyard. Pseudohome away from home. The pseudoextended family.

When your first child reaches first grade, it is like a divorce in the family. The public school gets custody and parents get visiting rights. It's really quite astonishing that the vast majority of the North American populace would give up the guardianship of their children so willingly and without so much as a fuss, let alone a fight.

School not only takes but is given the power over parenting children. The custodial pseudoparent/family school takes over when your child reaches five or six and many public schooling officials and experts have been trying for years to lower that magic mandatory age number to three, two, or even less.

Your children gone from their home and family, seven to nine hours a day (dependent upon whether or not they have to bus it to school), five days a week, nine to ten months of the year, twelve to thirteen years of their young lives. There are many educationers who are pushing the all-year plan ahead and this year-round schooling has already been implemented as pilot projects in some North American cities. Parents who want baby-sitters through the summer embrace such projects. Parents who want to protect their children should expel them.

Some say working parent families need their kids in school year-round, because no-one is around to watch the kids. When accused of running a glorified daycare, they retort with claims that children lose the September through May/June knowledge during the summer holiday, so they should all be in summer school so they won't forget what they've learned for the nine to ten months they've been in during the two to three they are out.

When my oldest son was in the public school system, I quickly found that life as we knew it ceased until the summer holiday finally rolled around. Mornings were spent sending him off to school and evenings were spent winding him down from school. I was lucky enough to enjoy a quick lunch with him at noon, because we lived in walking distance of the schools he attended during his short two and a half years in the system.

The noon lunch thing was perhaps more an annoyance than a pleasure though, because it broke up the day for me, waiting for my son's arrival or picking him up, feeding him in a flash and a flurry and then rushing him back. Noon didn't count for much except indigestion for both of us. I understood why so many mothers opted for the school lunch program if it was available.

Since children sleep eight to twelve hours at night, depending on their ages and individual needs, there are from twelve to sixteen waking hours left of the twenty-four day/night. Kids are gone to school from seven to nine hours a day and several hours are spent getting ready to go, winding down from and doing home work from school and then there's eating too.

If your child sleeps an average of ten hours a night, is gone to school for an average of eight hours, spends two hours eating and getting ready for school in the morning and another two doing homework from school and eating dinner at night, not to mention a meager two hours watching television; you are down to zero hours of quality time with which to spend together.

I know families and situations which are worse than this not so bad average. The kids are wakened out of their sleep to gulp down a quick and fairly empty breakfast, rushed off for a one hour bus-ride to school and then, ten hours later, arrive home for a late quick and fast supper, rush through the homework, and fall into bed exhausted. Sometimes there is time for a little TV, but time spent as a family getting to know each other better is difficult to find. The weekends offer some quality time, sometimes.

Parents who are a part of the public school system have little more than glorified visiting rights. The public school has control of the custody situation. The parents must revolve around the school. The school becomes the authority over the family. I once discovered that I could not, as a parent, legally retrieve my son from the school during school hours without the school's okay. My child was not my own until the school's-out buzzer sounded. My son was the school's and I was just the mother.

Just the mother. The title, "Mother," used to mean so much more in years of yesterday. So did "Father." They mean little today and they may mean even less tomorrow. There are many educationers who are really executioners in disguise. They want to execute the family as we've known it, as some of us still know it. One breed of social and political reformers or another, out to make us all good state zombies. Today they zombify the children, tomorrow, the world.

These educational and political elite, plan to control not only every school classroom, but every family home and eventually, every woman's womb. Through some of these outreach programs and other such helpful sounding services, so-called professional parent-teachers, go into homes to help parents parent their children, whether the parents or children want or need their brand of help or not.

These professional parent-teachers want more power to remove children who are not being raised to the state's satisfaction. Some social workers already do. Children have been removed for months or more, simply because a social worker suspects some kind of supposed abuse (such as breast-feeding one's baby as sexual abuse). The parents are guilty until they can prove themselves innocent. The parents and children are both abused severely in the process. At the very least, they are all scarred for life.

These professional parents want the power to giveth or taketh away parenting rights totally. Without a parenting diploma or degree, no couple would be granted permission to have or at least keep their baby. Without complying with the guidelines of the state parental planners, no couple would be allowed to keep their children. No family would be free. No couple would be free. No individual would be free.

So many of these social reformers plan their war against society and especially its families, in order to reform it to their theoretical visions of a greater good and a family of the state. They share their vision behind pleasant philosophies of equality and fair play, ending poverty and other niceties. They do their dirty work behind closed doors, hidden in lengthy lawyerese bills and proposals for change, and presented to the public with smiling faces.

Take a good look at your family. It is on the endangered list. The families of yesterday and today will be extinct if the family reformers have their way. Some families like mine refuse to feed the hands that bites us. We opt out of the public school banquet and all its programs. We hope our children will follow in our quest to save our family, generation upon generation, and that others will do the same. The world needs families. Real families, not state-formed pseudofamilies.

10. WOUNDS

As one of many millions of baby-boomers growing up in the public school, what I knew seemed normal and therefore, natural. As human beings, we can accustomize ourselves to many unnatural or unhealthy experiences. It is our survival instincts that help us to adapt to so many situations. Children growing up in ghettos can survive. Children in refugee camps can. Children who are being verbally, physically, or even sexually abused, can and do survive.

In surviving Hell or a Holocaust, though, there is a price to be paid. Survivors have scars. Handicaps. They end up less than they could have been. They start adulthood with less than they should have and it may take a lifetime to compensate for their losses.

As illiteracy rates scare us all into asking what is wrong with the public school systems, home schooled children are teaching themselves to read naturally. As vandalism destroys home and school property and violence in public schools attack students and teachers alike, home schooling families enjoy peace and love at home like the parents never knew in their childhoods.

There is a great divide. The division between the publicly-schooled and the home-schooled is growing. While the public schooling system is tearing families apart like never before, the home schooling homes are uniting parents and children in a lifetime bond.

Because of the public school experience, children are inflicted with wounds that must be healed. Where can they go to find healing? Religions offer healing of souls. Therapists offer healing of minds. Families offer healing of hearts.

I knew a man who chose to become a therapist simply because he saw the vast baby-boomer market of mix-ups. He was not a kind or caring man. He was more messed-up than most of us. He is just cashing in on all the pain. He works with the psychologically wounded. They go to him to get healed. Knowing him as I do, I pity the people who he supposedly helps.

There are good therapists who help those who seek it. As in all professions, there are good and bad. I have known too many people going into a profession for all the wrong reasons . . . Boys became doctors for the money, not to help sick people get well. Girls became nurses to meet and marry doctors and their money. Men and women became teachers for the easier hours and many paid holidays. One clean-cut, clean-shaven guy became a cop so he could advance his profitable life of drug-dealing. One womanizing, pornography-addicted doctor became a gynecologist for his own self-stroking perverted reasons. Pedophiles aspired to work with children for the easy access to their victims. When the wrong people enter any profession for the wrong reasons and especially perverted and evil ones, the result is as if a virus or a disease permeates that profession.

In the helping professions, there are those who help, but there are also those who hinder or even hurt or harm in their curing efforts. Prevention is the final cure. Home schooling offers prevention against the ills of the public school, and the public school cannot seem to cure its own ills.

Public school may be a necessity for some, but it is a child-watch service with high costs. Its supposed purpose, to educate the masses, is swallowed up by the child-care service it provides. As a child-care service, it is a sad substitute for home and family.

What the world needs now, more than ever, is love. Love from parents and family. The family must prevail over the public school that seeks to replace it. The state needs to get out of the childrearing business. It has failed the children far too long. The public schooling inflicted wounds could be prevented with a healthy dose of family and home. Home schooling is the remedy.

For those who have been wounded by the public school, it's time to take your children home and care for your wounds. In time they can heal.

HOME SCHOOLING, NATURALLY

11. SOCIALIZATION

Many of us home schooling parents are asked more and more, "What about the socialization your children are missing out on?"

When we first began home schooling, ten plus years ago, legalities and academics were the first concerns of those who questioned us. Socialization was lower down on the list. These days, socialization is almost, if not always, the first and foremost question on the minds of those curious about home schooling.

Most people now know that home schooling is a legal educational alternative. And the academics are academic. Almost everyone takes it for granted that children can learn more in a home school than in a public school now (that's how bad the public schools are doing). Who would argue now, that children could do without all the sex, drugs and violence that run rampant in the schools? Few do. But most people still want to know how our home schooled kids will get socialized properly at home.

What surprises me greatly is that in a country where socialism and communism has been feared, fought against and is now found out for what a failure and nightmare it has been (the U.S. much more so than Canada); socializing in the public school is highly prized (Canada much more so than the U.S.). To paraphrase Karl Marx, "one of the first steps to bringing a country to communism is bringing the children to public school." I see the socialism question as a pretty scary one.

When those curious, critical or concerned individuals quiz me on home schooling's lack of socialization, I always have at least a few answers that stump them. First I mention that most of public school's socialization is antisocialization or negative socialization. No one contests that. Next, I explain how my children can choose plenty of quality friends (versus quantity, at school) from among those in our neighborhood and from many sources through other activities beyond our city block. No one argues. Then I describe the family, both immediate and extended, as the basic social unit of society, where our children are getting the most natural and ideal socialization possible. No one pursues.

All that is necessary for the natural socialization of children is a community's basic societal group: the family. Even a family group so small as to consist of a mother and child, would be capable of providing the nurturing and guiding environment necessary to produce a properly socialized child.

Activities external to the family or home, such as after-school or summer-time neighborhood play; boy scouts or girl guides; church activities; dance, music or art classes; community teams; and so forth; provide opportunities for meeting friends. While we have always allowed our children time for outside socialization, we always came back to limiting it out of necessity.

All our children have demonstrated "negative sociability" or "peer-dependence syndrome" symptoms when their time with friends became too frequent or prolonged. We learned to limit their "outside contact" to maximize our children's positive or natural sociability within our home and ultimately elsewhere. As backward as the concept may seem to most, limiting social contact between children translates to more sociable kids.

Personality has a great deal to do with how sociable a child is or wants to be as well. The differences in degree of so-called sociability amongst our four children is amazing, considering the protected stable home environs they've all shared. Birth order could play a role as well as genetics. Three out of four of our children have always been generally outgoing and keen to make friends, while one has preferred to play shy. Why? I have a few theories.

One theory that stands out as clear as fact surrounds an experience with a child we took care of for a time. This boy decided to attempt a coup against our younger son. They were the same age and this little boy wanted to take our son's place in the family. He spoke of it openly as he attempted physical overthrow of our son. He asked to be called by our son's name. He spoke of his wish for our son to die and even seemed to attempt assassination as he attacked our son.

If the mother of this boy hadn't been my good friend in need, I would have stopped this child's care even sooner. By the time I finally did so, some damage had already been done. Left with some physical and emotional scars, this son of ours had little desire to play with boys his own age for months to years. This type of socialization is precisely what exists in daycares and schools. That's socialization.

For many of us home schoolers, socialization is or becomes the most important reason to keep kids out of the public schools. While there are many reasons people decide to keep, pull or yank their kids out of school; the stark contrast of the public school's socialization agenda to the natural socialization within the family home becomes so apparent as to shock.

Home schooling's opportunities for family home and community socialization offer such pleasant surprises, that looking back at the public school's socialization experiences look like a crime against nature.

Children don't come to this planet in litters of thirty, or even twenty or fifteen. It is true they occasionally come in groups of two, rarely three and very rarely (and nearly always due to unnatural fertility drugs) more; but the norm and what is natural is for children to be born one at a time.

Other intelligent creatures of this planet, such as chimpanzees and dolphins (generally all apes and whales), naturally space their babies four and five years apart. This is nature's design to allow the mother enough time to properly socialize her child and then her other children into her society.

While I wanted to space my children more like unto the chimpanzees I'd heard of, birth control doesn't always control birth for all of us, so I had three of my four babies in the space of four years. There were and are still many more challenges due to the closeness of those three of our children that aren't as pronounced as those between the two who are more than five years apart, but the sibling rivalry between our group of three is a breeze compared to what goes on between a group of thirty rivaling children in a classroom of a public school.

Combine the student rivalry with the insecurity the children feel because they are not in the comforting walls of their own home and near the comforting arms of their own family, and you get a sort of super rivalry. Children in classrooms are all vying for the love and affection of one teacher, a parent figure who may or may not care to love one or more of them. All but a few teacher's pets will inevitably be left out in the cold. As loving as some teachers may be, the chances of a teacher loving all thirty of her students equally well are dismally low. The chance of each and every child feeling loved adequately is less than zero and then some.

How much love is there from teachers when there is no pay offered?

Zero. How much is a mother paid to love her children? Zero. How many mothers love without being paid to do so? Millions. How many teachers go on strike when they are not given the pay raises they request or even demand? Millions.

Children are smart enough to know that if a teacher demands pay for her services, there is only room for so much love. True love is financially free. Every time teachers strike for increased pay, their students are reminded that teachers teach for the money. Some believe in what they do too, but it is a job and a career. It is not a relationship. Teachers are not mothers. Their students are not their children. No matter how many times they might think it, wish it, feel it or say it; it is simply not true.

As much as I feel that one teacher training a pack of thirty children all at once is terribly unnatural, very inadequate, and awfully saddening, perhaps I wouldn't think it was so bad if parents had a little say in the matter. If the public schools were training society's children with methods and curriculum that reflect society's parents, maybe it wouldn't be such a dismal failure, not to mention a near complete undermining of parental authority.

As the years have gone by, the schooling authorities have leached more and more authority away from parents, and if that isn't bad enough, they want ever more. They want to bleed parents dry. To death, in fact. There are many school reformers who are bent on extracting everything but wombs, through ever younger mandatory school entrance ages, universal daycares, outreach programs (where teacher-types reach into homes to scold parents), social working (removal of children from supposedly offending parents) and parental diplomas or degrees, required by prospective parents (state permission for parenting).

I have often thought, or at least hoped, that this downward social evolutionary trend at the public school was a pitiful accident. I surmised that the socializing of school children breeds socialism in the adults they grow to become, and then little by little, generation upon generation, socialism grows, an unchecked noxious weed. Unfortunately, I don't think it is an accident. The more I read, see and hear, the more evidence I find of a very deliberate push towards socialism and then communism, by political, social and school reformers who cannot get their socialist and then communist way honestly through clear votes of North American people.

Since, like in Russia, a revolution didn't bring socialism to North America, the people wouldn't, and brute force couldn't, all the reformers cleverly decided to sneak socialism in through various channels. Channel number one: namely, the public schools, where parents thought their children were safe and sound. Most especially, parents thought their children were learning. Learning their ABC's and the three R's and all the academic basics they needed to get to college and/or university. Or at least to get a good job, if not a higher-learning-based career.

What kids of North America have been taught is more and more how to be a cog in the state wheel and less and less how to read, write and calculate. State-schooled students are losing their ability to learn on their own, think for themselves and come up with creative ideas. Many have learned to be good state zombies and that's exactly what the socialist reformers want.

When my eldest son was in school ten years or so ago, the area he did least well in was the social one, according to some of his teachers. He didn't stand in line well (he stood in his own way), he put his hand up for every question (he always had an answer), he didn't usually follow other children (he was always leading them), he was free-spirited (he did not easily conform) and he didn't always obey every rule (he didn't bow down to injustices). Such individualism, leadership and enthusiasm for learning and socializing becomes a problem for the teacher who is trying to control a large group of children who are dying to be free again (that's what summer holidays are all about).

Most teachers tend to like those children who fill the bulk of the bell curve: the ones in the middle or the mediocre masses. They offer the least challenge to the teacher. Teachers like average kids. They stand in line well, they conform, they don't stand out, they sit still, they speak when spoken to, they are seen but not heard and they fit into the group. The more or less gifted kids are on the outside of the group. Public schools are about groups, not individuals. Just when my son began to succumb to the state school ways and fit into the group, we found home school and then he was free to be home free again.

State schools offer new freedom. The kids have also been taught how to be sexually free. Free from responsibilities and commitments. Free from parental permissions. But not free from sexually transmitted diseases (many incurable) or pregnancies and too many subsequent abortions. All these freedoms (promiscuity) and counterfreedoms (diseases and pregnancy) are on the increase within the youth populous, in direct proportion to the amount of money spent on sexual education in those areas. Called sexual education by its authors, or sexual miseducation by many parents, lessons on sex are peddled to public schools' kids through so much pornography, in some forms, that any clear-thinking individual would call sexual abuse.

If any parent forced their children to engage in the activities common to the state's sexual education classes, their children could and would be removed by the state for sexual abuses. Sex education teachers promote (even to the point of coercion and force) the following as sexual edification for the young (as early as kindergarten): viewing pornographic movies (some are hardcore), playing with sex toys (such as extremely realistic models of genitalia, including those of the erect variety), studying sexual paraphernalia (including tasting new condom flavors) and exploring alternative orientations (from foreplay options and multitudinous positionings to pushing and shoving homosexuality and mocking monogamous marriage and even encouraging animal experimentation).

What is good for the state is not so for the parent. There are few parents who would want to subject their children to anything near the sexual embarrassment, humiliation, and misinformation in the name of sexual education that the state's schools shove down little throats, but if any tread even near, they would be guilty of sexual abuse. Sexual education teachers are guilty of sexual abuse. Public schools and their officials are guilty of sexually abusing the young in their charge. These abuses abound.

My socialization point about all this sex education is that much of the sexual socializing the state schools are doing is sexual antisocialization. Kids grow up with emotional, social and sexual problems precisely because of what their teachers teach them about sex. They don't learn about love, commitment, responsibility, honesty, monogamy, marriage, fidelity, family, or anything else that through a natural and healthy design is all intertwined. When sex is subtracted from life, removed from natural living as a subject and then is injected into the public school, it becomes and is the lowest common denominator. Something purely physical. Worse than animal.

Animals instinctually reproduce. Their sexual drive propels them no further than what is necessary to further their species. Human beings have a constant and consistent drive that needs positive socializing to tame it lest it go wilder than the wild. Sexual deviancy and misery is not what society needs more of. The public school socialization is giving license to a dangerous sexuality which has a serious impact on the social side of society (not to mention the physical health side).

Thankfully, it is in our nature to rise above the negative. Many manage to do so. Many of those who were abused (emotionally, physically or sexually) as children rarely go on to abuse. Some, for some reason, do.

Most adults can overcome the group mentality of the public school once grown up and out of it. Many of us grew up to stand tall against peer-dependence and peer-pressure. Even some gang members have grown towards better, beyond their gangs. It seems to be quite difficult for a small majority or at least a very loud minority. The media is by and large a part of that minority and we hear that side so much and so very loudly because they have the power to voice it.

Think about the children who grow up in public school, go to college, and to university and then return to public school to become teachers. It's a cycle and perhaps in many cases, a vicious one. Anyone who never lives beyond the unnatural and unreal world of the public school never gets terribly in touch with reality (the same goes for the people who graduate from school and go straight to government work and politics). Perhaps the reason many media-ites seem so socialistic is because they go from the socialist state of the state school into a similar state of affairs within the media.

Free enterprise is the natural and real world and public institutions (schools and any other government department) have very little, if anything, to do with freedom or enterprise. Public institutions are of a contrived world. The public world cannot stand on its own without the dollars that it sucks out of the free enterprise world: the pockets of the people who work at real wealth-generating jobs.

The good social behavior most of us desire of ourselves, our children and our neighbors should not be confused with the socializing of the schools, social programs or socialism. Socialism is at war with freedom. It always has and it always will be. Freedom respects the individual's rights and responsibilities. Socialism seeks to subjugate everyone and everything in its path.

Tomorrow's society would be far better off without today's state school socialization. Public school socialization produces an antisocial product. It may be a socialistic product, but that is not a social one. Picture every youth counterculture you've ever witnessed. Remember gangs. Think of groupies. All these are caused by peer-dependence and the state school variety of socialization.

Nature's way is the family way—the social order of the family. The good social behavior most parents instill in their children is based on the society they want to remain a part of: the extended family, the friends and neighbors, the community, and beyond. Parents and their children, usually have natural incentives to be socialized, or civilized. This natural socialization is positive socialization. It grows naturally and need not be state-engineered in order to grow better. Family-based socialization is the most successful socialization.

12. LEGALIZATION

Picture yourself with your newborn cradled in your arms. Advance the film so you can watch the first steps your child takes, then hear the first words and then imagine all the firsts. Now try to feel all the excitement and joy that is yours as a parent to your own children. Who knows such strong feelings of love and fulfillment? Only other parents for their own children.

Now sense how you feel about someone kidnapping your child. How would you react to seeing your child ripped out of your life for hours, days, weeks, months or even years? You would be outraged. You would do all in your power to bring your child back into your home where she or he belongs, where love for him or her abounds.

The public school kidnaps children, confines them, brainwashes them and then lets you visit them, having taught your children to spy on you. That's an extreme way of looking at what the schools do. A kinder way to see it is that the public school is a universal child care system that we all pay for and therefore must all use. It's a glorified service at best.

What is legal? Should a forced child detention center be legal while raising children at home is not? Mandatory schooling was supposed to secure equal opportunity for education for every child. Public schooling doesn't do that. Mandatory schooling was also implemented to get kids out of the streets. It doesn't even do that. Truancy among publicly schooled kids has always been a problem.

Public schooling has taken the mass majority of children out of their homes, for no gain in education and it certainly hasn't cleaned up the streets. Home schooling opponents don't even argue the educational aspects anymore. Too many public schools have failed children as the children fail and too many home schooled kids are excelling.

Home schooling critics always seem to hang onto the socialization consideration. But, they say, the children will be social rejects. They won't fit in. They won't conform. They won't be like everybody else. Good, I say. They'll do what they believe in. They'll have minds of their own. They'll lead where others will follow.

The legal opportunities to home school grow as the movement explodes across North America. It has always been legal one way or another. As difficult as some schooling officials have tried to make it, there have always been ways and means for home schoolers. There are loopholes and parents seem to find them. There are also provisions for kids who cannot go to school, confined to bed, home or hospital because of sickness, and must school away from school. There are private schools. Some home schoolers use rulings already in place and then others fight for new ones.

In the more than ten years since we began home schooling our children, I have seen the home schooling movement go from a legally trepidous one, to one where it is now on firm legal grounds. Back when we began, families like us carefully wrote letters informing schooling authorities of our home schooling intentions, hoping to get lost in the paperwork of a massive institution.

Those who feared noncooperation of school boards, just hid out and waited in their little home schooling foxholes hoping to survive until times changed. Many home schoolers shared methods to avoid detection. I called it closet home schooling. Some called it going underground.

From time to time we would anxiously read or hear of a home schooling family being taken to court, or worse yet, their children being taken away. Some families moved away from school boards intent on using litigation to stop them from home schooling their children. Sometimes they had to move more than once.

More often than not, public schools left known home schoolers alone, simply because the publicity of a fight would cast a negative shadow on the state-run schools. Those home schooling parents who might look good on camera were left alone. Occasionally, the state would find a family that would not look quite so good on camera. That's when the talons came out. Outlandish unsympathetic caricatures (drug-junky or religious-cult types) would be attacked. The state wanted sympathy for its supposed cause: saving the children.

In spite of direct resistance and discouragement from public schools, the numbers of home schooling families continued to climb and the state schooling officials wanted to deal with the problem. Rather than openly fight against an obvious force to be reckoned with, some public schools began to cooperate with home schooling families. In some cases it became almost trendy to cooperate: pilot projects and the like. Some so-called educational experts even like to think it was all their idea: alternatives in education with titles like The Year 2000 Program, which is one new method of tomorrow much like many home schools of yesterday.

Some home schoolers believe the evidence points to the money trail. The more families opted out of the public school system, the less was the state school budget. Every child that registers in a public school translates to more than $6000 education money each year. Every time a parent decided to home school a child, there was minus $6000 for a school in that area. The numbers of home schoolers were growing each year as the dollar figures were going down, enough so that some schooling officials noticed the falling money or lack thereof.

And speaking of money, I love to remind myself of the fact that every year I continue to home school my four children, I save taxpayers more than $24,000 (4 times $6000 equals $24,000). When my four kids are finished schooling, I will have saved my fellow taxpayers approximately $300,000 or more. For every child who is home schooled for 12 (grades 1 through 12) to 14 (kindergarten through 13th grade) years, taxpayers are saved $72,000 to $84,000 total. Every time a family commits to home schooling, taxpayers begin to save. These figures should make the general public receptive. Of course these numbers aren't shown to the public by the public school authorities.

Beyond a more receptive public at large, home schoolers have found more receptivity from the public schools, in recent years. Many will allow children to go part time for certain subjects or activities. Some have given learning allowances (from mostly pittance to generous amounts some of the time). Others will give supplies. Through it all, more often than not, the school gets far more out of the deal than the student. More money means more self-perpetuation.

Many home schooling children are registered under private schools instead. Others are still unregistered. Those home schooling families who remain underground or in the closet need not necessarily fear, for the public school is fighting for life and breath and has little energy left to hassle with home schoolers who are proving themselves more capable than products of the state system.

When the state has taken families to court, families have often won. When they lose they can take the case higher. Many families who find themselves under fire have just moved to where the home schooling grass is greener.

With such high failure rates, the public school has little legal clout against home schoolers who have such great track records to draw upon. Home schoolers have been happy to see the state giveth a little on the home schooling front. But, what the state giveth, the state can taketh away. If that day shall come again, home schoolers will find ways and means as they always have.

Home schooling has become so popular and so pervasive among the masses in the last few years that it would be extremely difficult to eradicate it, even if the state should try.

13. THE THREE R'S

Back when girls stayed home and boys took tutors or went to school part-time, the three R's became the standard schooling fare. Basic education covered the basics: Reading, wRiting and aRithmetic. After schools of boys began to see girls in the schools too, the educational basics began to see learning luxuries added. Many frivolous extras were added, always at taxpayers' expense and usually without their permission.

As illiteracy rates soared in and after schools, there came a nationwide panic. Public schools began to phase out the frills in favor of the basics in education. The narrow focus of the three R's was brought back into focus.

As educational extremists on opposite sides of fences fight over what is green, many parents want to get back to the basics rather than fight over what books should be banned from the schools. Too much money and time has already been spent teaching kids things many of their parents don't think they need or ought to know.

Too many theories have been taught as facts and too many opinions have been taught as truths. Why did we begin to have and pay for public schools? To promote philosophies? To socialize? To further socialism? To push theories and press opinions into children's brains? No. To give every individual an equal chance at an education. To educate. To educate for what purpose? To further the state?

The only educational thing most parents and educational advocates might agree on are the basics, which are the only essentials needed. All learning that comes after, should be the choice of the learner. In other words, if kids learn to read, write and calculate at basic levels, they can then go on, on their own from there, and they do. Some kids go from walking and talking to reading and writing and then calculating on their own. Self-taught kids exist. They have learned by example. They watch and copy until they get it right.

If you walk around children, they learn to walk. If you talk to children, they learn to talk. If you read to children, they learn to read. If you write around children, they learn to write. If you calculate around children, they learn to calculate. That's the natural way.

Whether or not children have been self-taught or just taught the basics of reading, writing and arithmetic; once they have the basics, they have a solid foundation to stand on. Once they know the language of our written world, they can enter it and partake. That's the natural way for kids to progress, learning by watching and doing, through questions and answers and most especially, choosing for themselves as they go and grow.

14. THE THREE A'S

Rather than seeing learning basics as the old fashioned three R's, I like to see it as the three A's. By replacing Reading, wRiting and aRithmetic with Academics, Athletics and the Arts, learning is more a part of life and life is more learning. While the three A's are by no means everything we need to learn in life, they replace the three R's and many of the extras found in the schools.

The Academics exercise the left side of the brain for the most part, Athletics give the body a healthy workout and the Arts exercise the right side of the brain, so we're told. Thought-provoking/memorizing/problem solving abilities grow through language, math and sciences within Academics. Agility, dexterity and strength improve in Athletics. Creativity blossoms and thrives within the Arts.

Not only do the three A's offer a sound educational base for the learner, but this system appeases the public schooling officials, who want to know that the home schooling student is receiving comparable education to what is offered in the nearby public school.

Parents have the opportunity to offer their children the three A's within their home, fine-tuned to their life-styles and beliefs. Parents can offer opportunities but in the end, children will decide what they study, and will learn what they want to learn. Whatever a parent or teacher teaches a child, the child will learn what the child will learn. Whether or not a parent or teacher teaches a child, the child will learn what the child will learn.

Learning is an individual thing, it is a private affair. You may teach a concept or a skill but you cannot really force or even give it. The learner must receive. The learner must learn. Learners are really their own best teachers.

In the following three chapters, I will share some experiences within our own home school as examples of learning within the three A's. I always see learning as life, and life as learning. While I separate learning into subjects so you can begin to see what I am trying to say, I always end up seeing learning as a whole. We can dissect it into parts to understand it, but when learning lives, it is whole.

15. ACADEMICS

(Language, Math, Sciences)

Language

Language Immersion

In Canada, French immersion classes are in vogue. Even immigrants from Central America, South America, Eastern Europe, the British Isles and so on enroll their children in French immersion classes. Some of these kids think it is cool to speak French (even to the rejection of their language of origin—especially when English is their second language and then French their third). Some kids hate French because they are being forced to live with it constantly in school (even to the point of rebelling against the language and despising all French Canadians).

The French language is supposed to give children future advantage in their Canadian careers. Past Prime Minister Pierre Elliot Trudeau made sure this was true in the governmental sector. His language legacy has ensured that those who are fluent in the French language (the fluency tests are so difficult and updated they can only be passed by those using French on a daily basis) outweigh the English in the federal government, and most especially in the higher levels of country control.

This was all a part of Trudeau's plan to "frenchify" Canada. Federal bilingualism entrenched French beyond Quebec into all of Canada. French immersion in the schools is supposed to further the French language further. This is a French perpetuation policy that has hurt Canada. It has divided Canada into warring French and English camps. Some call for similar programs and plans for Spanish in the U.S.

I have heard good and bad things about the French immersion programs from both parents and children. On the negative side, in some cases, speaking French is top priority, even if the studies suffer, often severely; and some kids lose marks or percentage points on their grades if they are caught speaking anything but French at school. On the positive side, some parents feel their kids are removed from the public school at large by being placed in a special program which stands apart like French immersion does; and this is somewhat true, sometimes, in Catholic schools, where studies are patterned after parents beliefs more.

Who would argue that learning more than one language is a good thing? I certainly wouldn't. The more languages one knows, the more advantage one has in our smaller and smaller world. Who would argue that when one is immersed in a language, one learns it faster and better? That's how kids learn their mother language; from their mother as she speaks her mother's tongue to her own children.

Beyond the problems inherent with the unnatural public school, I wonder at parents who send their children off to school to learn another language (especially one they do not know or understand at all). I wonder if they know even less of what their children are being taught because it is in a foreign tongue (some of these kids love to use their *secret* language around their parents who are out in the language cold, often mocking them in secret). My question to them would be, why not learn another language together, as a family?

There are many home schooling families who have brought more than one foreign language into their home to learn as a family together: Japanese, Chinese, Russian, and the list could go on. Beyond the home schooling realm, some people have been bringing back languages from their past, the languages of their mothers' and fathers' generations before them. Some of the languages are obscure and some are even endangered. Such languages as Sioux and Welsh are making comebacks. This is all of the people, by the people, for the people.

When the government (usually pursued and then pulled by special interest groups — the minority controlling the majority again) promotes a program, it is more often than not a government-perpetuating program. Programs cost money, costing taxpayers, perpetuating government power, and hurting the future further. These government controlled movements are unnatural and unhealthy.

When a family decides to implement a program into their lives, it is a natural move. When an individual decides to learn something, it is a natural choice. When someone decides to learn another language, there must be enough desire to accomplish it. Many children have learned other languages in (through books, tapes or videos) or beyond (outside classes or tutorage) their own home schools.

Cultural Language

Multicultural programs are another politically popular thing in Canada (advancing the supposed Canadian cultural mosaic that exists mostly in theorists heads). Again, I am all for cultural diversity and promotion, but not by the government and not to the tune of tax dollars. When the big government starts throwing money at special cultural interest groups, cultural group envy and tug of wars begin.

There are plenty of examples of cultural and ethnic groups who do well at perpetuating themselves with no tax dollars nor governmental programs. Culture actually is more of a spontaneous and natural result of family and community cohesion. When the government gets involved, there is an agenda from above.

Many home schools do what most other homes do: advance the culture of their choice within their own home. Parents lean toward one culture or another and as the children grow, they do too.

We found that as children grow up, they often yearn for more than what has been offered them in their own home and family. As I looked back with pride toward some of my recent cultural heritage and my husband his, our eldest son began to look beyond ours, back even further. So began our son's own self-chosen Celtic cultural course.

While I was concentrating on cowboys, Indians, pioneers, pilgrims and early explorers of North America, my son yearned for more. He went back to the British Isles for our source, the Celts. The whole family has been edified as he shared from all he was learning about our own family's roots.

I was taught little about my own personal heritage through the public school as a child. What I learned came from my family and church and then I began learning on my own, following my cultural yearnings.

As human beings it is natural for us to yearn for culture. Present culture and past culture. I have always enjoyed looking to other cultures for ideas and lessons in life: what seems to work and what doesn't. Much of it can be very entertaining too: the foods and clothing, the songs and dances, the costumes and the decor. In North America, diverse cultures are everywhere. We are free to sample them as we wish. Culture is free for the partaking.

Religious Language

Whether your spirituality leads you to God through one religion or another, you should be free to follow where you choose. Each family should be spiritually free from the state. Unfortunately, in North America, the religion of *Secular Humanism* is being promoted vigorously by governments through public schools and other arms of the state power and influence.

Natural spirituality grows through the individual, family, church, community and then country. Upward, growing spontaneously. Not downward, being pushed and shoved, pressured and coerced. State religion is more than unnatural; it is unhealthy and even deadly to freedom.

Many families have chosen home schooling simply because of their religious principles. Since the Constitution (backed by the powerful special interest groups again) took Judeo-Christian or Bible-based religion as we knew it out of the public schools and substituted atheism and other assorted theories, many families felt they had no choice but to enroll their kids almost anywhere else. Those who couldn't find or afford a private school or religious school that was compatible to their own spiritual beliefs in their area, had to turn to other alternatives.

Protestant parents have even sent their kids to Catholic schools in order to save them from the atheistic public schools. Christian schools have flourished in recent years. Other religious schools are sprouting and growing as well. Increasing numbers of families have found that home schooling is a perfect alternative: a tailor-made religiously compatible opportunity.

Religion is the language of the soul and we all should be free to exercise the freedom of our souls. The only way you can share your soul with your children is to share your religious beliefs with them. When they are grown, they will choose their own. If they have grown close to you, they will not go far from you.

The Secret World of Words

First, children conquer to some degree, the spoken language, their mother tongue. Everyone agrees that children teach themselves to talk. Infants have proven themselves worthy of this challenge and so no classes are prepared for teaching them. Not yet, or at least not universally. It is for reading and writing that schools stake a claim for their initial existence.

Unfortunately, more for the kids than for the schools, schools can't guarantee that reading and writing will be given to the children. Not even to the vast majority. To move from the spoken to the written language, each child must find their own individual bridge. Learning the written language is as personal a task as learning the spoken.

Our written language, a somewhat hidden language, is a language kids beg us to share with them. It doesn't take kids long to figure out that there is a language of symbols, a language in code that the adults use somewhat in secret. The written language intrigues even tiny children: they want to know what this is all about! Once children have deciphered our spoken tongue they set about deciphering our written language in much the same way. This task is more difficult than the first one, to be sure, but, they can do it with little or even no help.

Of course, it is better for them if we try to help when we can, when they want us to. By acting as teaching guides, we can make the task of learning the written language easier for them. When my kids come to me with a question about how a word is spelled, I just answer them. I don't get them to try to sound it out or do anything else that will make them feel embarrassed, tested, inferior or stupid. I try to aid them similarly to how I did when they were learning to talk.

I don't know if there is anything more thrilling than watching one's children grow and learn in a healthy and natural way. It is a gleefully joyful experience at least. In our home, for learning there are no deadlines, no tests, no expectations. We simply wait and watch the process unfold like a breathtaking piece of costly material. A work of art and science. A natural wonder. Unfolding like a rose.

Mommi? Draw Some Words For Me

"Mommi? Can you draw for me? I don't want pictures this time." My four year old daughter announced, "I want you to draw me some words so I can pretend to be a Mommi."

"Oh." I understood, I thought, "You mean you want to pretend to write books like Mommi does?"

"Yep. So draw some words for me, Mommi. Right now, Okay?"

"Okay sweetie. Just tell me the story and I'll write it down for you."

"No, Mommi. Not a story. Just words."

"Okay. Tell me the words you want me to write for you."

"H. Q. R. S. T., H. A. B. C., Q. R. T., H. B. C . . . uh, . . . H. X. Y. Z . . . uh, um . . . "

"Those are letters, sweetie. Words are like: cat, dog, computer, hippopotamus and . . . "

"Okay, okay, Mommi . . . do the letters. I want you to draw me the letters in my book."

Well, I have to say that I had to pay attention and write the letters she asked for, because she'd probably have noticed if I had missed one or changed the order or anything not in keeping with her exact request. She did correct me on a few mistakes I made.

I would often think about times like that. While my six and seven year olds were definitely asking me for words and sentences, as they worked on their books, my four year old was asking for letters as well as numbers. My middle two children had the letters down, and now needed help in spelling words, my four year old couldn't quite write the letters herself yet, while she could recognize them to read them. She was in the middle of moving from reading letters in the alphabet to writing them.

Young Readers

All four of my children began reading or recognizing words at about the age of three. I tried the flash card routine with my eldest daughter for a few weeks or months to the point that she was reading a three hundred plus word set. Then I became too busy with my fourth baby to continue the program (she subsequently and fairly promptly forgot all I had taught her). With super-baby techniques I could have turned my babies into memorizing whiz kids, but I was awfully busy so I missed that possible opportunity. Sometimes I thought I had missed out when I missed the genius boat and other times I thought that the more natural approach float we stayed on might be best after all.

There are many who would argue the virtues of parent led learning games for little children to help them towards greater learning strides. But if a child chooses chewing on a rubber toy over playing a learning game his or her parent has planned, the child should have the right to choose to chew.

All debates on better-baby teaching methods aside, I was too busy trying to help feed, clothe and shelter our four kids to give them each the three ten-second memorization sessions a day to help them into the better-baby brain-child hall of fame. It wasn't the flashing time I couldn't find, so much as it was the time to make the hundreds and thousands of flash cards that were needed to feed my babies all those bits of intelligence.

Although I didn't offer my kids show-stopping, infant-reading opportunity for long, they've been enjoying learning to read little by little, here and there, and each at their own pace.

Without any lessons since our eldest son was helped to master "See Jane run, fall down go boom and Dick hop, skip, jump over Spot, the lazy dog who sleeps by the cute cat Puff," he has long since been an avid speedreader, much to the disgust of his friends. He is often called a walking encyclopedia, by his friends.

Our other three children are well into various stages of the reading experience, following their own curiosities towards mastering the written language as they did the spoken so well.

One note that is worth remembering while you watch and assist your children on the reading road: some children learn to read early and some learn to read late. If children are left to choose for themselves, many will choose to wait to learn to read. This can be quite trying for a parent who hasn't quite the faith to believe their child will manage reading like s/he did speaking.

Many kids would rather play than read, for a while and some for quite a while. I have read of many and met some home schooling kids who seemed to play until they were about twelve, the age that Raymond Moore (and others) says the intellectual mind comes together. If kids were allowed to choose for themselves when they would learn to read, I wonder if more would wait until so much later to do so.

For those parents who can't stand idly by and watch while their children play all their days away, sit and read to them, read with them and get them to read to you. Encourage them, applaud them, cheer them on. Share your reading world with them like you did your speaking world. Show them by reading things yourself. Children want to enter our worlds. If they choose to join us later, it doesn't mean they are slow.

Remember also that everyone has their strengths and weaknesses. Some are strong in reading abilities and some are strong in other areas. Part of learning, is learning your own strengths and how to apply them towards successes in your life. Not everyone was meant to be a doctor or a lawyer, a writer or an artist. But, everyone who can learn to speak can learn to read. They may just need a little more time or a little more help. Follow the reader, because the reader knows best.

The first three E's of education definitely apply to learning to read: example, example, example. If your kids never see you reading, they won't have as much a desire to pick up a book as they will if they see you immersed in books frequently. Read, and your children will want to follow your example.

The next three E's of education that can help kids learn to read are: excitement, encouragement and enlistment. Parents who love their children naturally get excited when their children progress in the reading world. Good parents encourage their children along the reading path. Responsible and concerned parents find that they sometimes must enlist their children to join in on some worthy activities, like reading. Late bloomers might need to be enlisted and encouraged with a good dose of excitement.

Some of us natural home schooling parents have felt that a few of our kids needed an extra boost along the reading road. Sometimes we are motivated because we feel a certain child needs that extra little push across that bridge that takes kids from talking to reading. Some feel pressured by family, friends, or neighbors who may critically look upon our "illiterate" children. Some just fear and want to protect their children from the public school's giant hand reaching in and grabbing them out of the home school.

One couple became concerned over their son who seemed not to have any intention of reading. He was verbally advanced for his age, but he was simply not reading. This boy loved to be read to, so his father decided that for every book he read to his son, his son must read one to him. In a few short weeks, this boy was well on his own way, bitten by the reading bug in a big way.

I reached a point where I decided that my three youngest kids needed some incentive to help in their reading adventures. Just as I laid out specific times for tasks before more pleasurable times, I did so for reading. There was work before play and healthy food before treats. We had snack time, teeth time, potty time, story time and hug time before bedtime, and then sleep time, a natural order of things.

In the reading department, there came a time when my three youngest kids just weren't. They were too busy playing and the oldest of the three was asking for more and more TV time. All I did was explain that there was a lack of reading among them, and then announced that from now on, there was to be reading time before TV time and that for every half hour of TV they wanted, they would each have to read a book of their choice to me. TV time went down and reading time went up. In a matter of weeks, they were reading books to each other, with little help and no assignments from me. They were across the bridge and on the reading road.

I believe we are all on the learning to read path. I'm still learning to understand, speak, read and spell new words. We all are. At least we should be. Once you've mastered one language, you could go on to the next.

What Does M.C.D.O.N.A.I.D.S Spell, Mom?

This next bit is my husband's favorite tidbit to rib me with, especially when we're out and we drive past a McDonald's. Our whole family was out and about in our new family van and while my husband and I were enjoying a conversation up front, our three youngest were interjecting with what-does-such-and-such-spell-Mom? questions as we passed by sign after sign.

Big stores, little stores, gas stations and stop signs; and then restaurant after restaurant. One of my little ones asked what M.C.D.O.N.A.I.D.S spelled and I answered, not having paid too close attention to the question and having my mind on my conversation, "McDodaids, sweetie."

My husband began to roar with laughter and commented, "Gee, honey, I feel so confident in your ability to teach our kids to learn to read. They'll go through life thinking that McDodaids has sold over a billion or so Big Macs and assorted other sandwiches."

It took me a moment to figure out the mistake: the L mistaken by a little one as an I and I thought the N was a D. It's explainable and forgivable but unforgettable. McDonald's is forever McDodaids in our family, even though the kids all know what the sign says now (a private joke shared to illustrate how children learn to read while they ride).

1-2-3-Ready, Set, Go!

1—READY: Reading Letters—learning the alphabet. As kids gradually learn to recognize each alphabet symbol, they begin to assimilate some sounds. It is not necessarily necessary for kids to learn the "sound" of each letter. They don't need to be taught each letter's sound to learn them over time. Learning the alphabet is not as crucial to the reading ability as many believe it to be. This should be a fun beginning, not a rote memorization one.

2—SET: Reading Words—learning words. Some kids only memorize whole words, while some only sound out each letter phonetically, and others do some combination of both. By offering children both options, we give them the best chance at feeling out their best reading course. Let them stumble and skip as they move forward, and they will.

3—GO: Reading Phrases—the reading process speeds up, as words become symbols beyond the letter symbols. Even and perhaps especially, little kids can memorize whole phrases from their favorite books (page after page after page) or other reading sources (packaging of toys and food or advertisements). Silent reading speeds reading. Only oral reading can slow the reading process, especially if kids continually learn by sounding out the words, letter by letter. Don't tie their hands by forcing them to read each word, one letter sound at a time. Set them free to skim over the words, picking up the message through context.

Read!

- **R**elax and reading will come easier, the more easy going you are.
- Enjoy the process. Reading is a natural process. It *can* come naturally.
- **A**llow kids the freedom to learn in their own way and at their own pace.
- **D**emonstrate reading to your kids by reading to them and on your own.

A, B, C . . .

Always make your home a house of learning: letters on the walls; words on furniture; names on persons, places and things; and books everywhere (but don't get neurotic about it). Supply paper and pencils to write with (coloring and drawing enhance fine motor skills and coordination and thereby enhance printing and writing abilities) and typewriters or computers for typing or word processing skills. Make reading time a time in every day, like food time, teeth time, cleaning time, cuddle time, TV time and sleep time. Remember, we live in a *textual* world. Opportunities for reading are all around us: labels, packaging, signs, advertising, and even TV.

Bridge the gap between talking and reading by shortening it. Make it easy for kids to learn to read. Equate how you helped them enter the world of the spoken word and you can help them enter the world of the written word, because it *is* such a similar process. Picture/word books help early readers: one picture, one word, per page. Kids can use these on their own. The picture symbol gives the clue to the word symbol, thus bridging the gap for the child. Even "word only" books can help the youngest readers to read, but you must sit and read the words to them, for a while. Little kids need BIG letters. Small text is hard on little less developed eyes and can cause the need for glasses. The older the kids, the smaller the text they can take.

Copying is the key to learning. Your kids copy you. If you read, your kids will want to read, too. Read to them, show them the words you are reading. Let them memorize in their own way: letter by letter, word by word, phrase by phrase. Share your favorite books with them and let them share their favorite books with you, allowing them to learn to read at their own pace. Never force or use any negative tactics, but instead, lead the way and they will follow.

Math

Kids Crave Collections

The child who is our greatest collection collector is also perhaps our greatest mathematical mind. The sorting, organizing and counting that usually accompanies the ownership of a collection of many things, affords the owner plenty of opportunity to solidify many basic mathematical concepts.

Again and again, I've watched our little collector count, line up, sort into various groups of similars and recount his numerous collections of little things, in particular. He has been the one most able to absorb and display a great understanding of many mathematical concepts from an early age. He is our most logical child. He takes after his father who did the same, collecting things throughout his childhood.

I once asked my little son why his favorite things were all little things. He told me that he liked little things because he could keep them with him. He carried two buckets of these little things around with him almost everywhere: to the washroom, to the table, to watch TV and to bed. At any time, he could sit down, sort, line up and count his collections, which he loved very much to do. He also mentioned that he was building the muscles in his arms by carrying his very heavy buckets of little things around with him.

It is quite a picture: this little curly-headed, chubby little guy carrying around these two large buckets full of little things. He had little people and animal figures, beads, rocks, puzzle pieces, cards, dice, paper, confetti, plastic and cardboard snippings, picture cutouts and so on. When I allowed him, he also carried around Lego® pieces and little building blocks, too.

Lego® Mania

There was once a learning program on PBS that focused on math. One of the highlights was a look at Lego® and how it helps kids to assimilate mathematical concepts as they play with a new toy every day.

The bricks come in ones and two's and three's and four's and more's. As kids build, they add and multiply there way to the top of their little buildings. Without even knowing they have entered the dreaded world of math, they are soaking in it.

Other building bricks are like that, too. The little red and white bricks I grew up on had a similar effect on me and the Lincoln Logs probably did too. The colors of Lego and others like them, create the opportunity or need for sorting in groups of color. Our children have logged hours of Lego building over the years and we were thrilled to find out that our investment in toys we all loved had been a learning one after all.

Measuring

Baking is more than all it's cooked up to be: One teaspoon, two tablespoons, three cups, four pounds; single, double, triple or quadruple the recipe. As you roll up your sleeves and dig into the kitchen, you're turned onto math before you turn on the oven.

Women in the kitchens have been better at math than they've been led to believe. While the experts told us women didn't have minds for math, women were using math in their kitchens to cook and bake for their families. And their children climbed on chairs beside them to learn math along with them.

The most memorable math classes ever held were held in a mother's kitchen. Who could forget a math lesson learned to the taste of a chocolate chip or oatmeal raisin cookie? Math never tasted so good.

Sewing is another math class. I started learning to love math designing and sewing for my doll more than twenty-five years ago. As I became more and more proficient at sewing design, I had to become more proficient in my math skills. Boys, as well as girls, can have fun with math in sewing design adventures.

Just give children measuring tapes and they go wild discovering how long, wide and tall things are. Weigh scales are more great learning fun. Anything that weighs or measures will offer hours of fun to a kid.

In measuring and all other mathematical pursuits you guide your children through, remember that creativity counts more than memorizing facts. As Albert Einstein once said, "Imagination is more important than knowledge." The man who created $E = MC2$, never memorized his own phone number because he didn't want to clutter his mind with facts that he could easily look up. I like to remember that.

Mouse Math

With the discovery of mice in our neighbors garage, a mathematical reaction was set in motion. They had moved from a farm some six months prior and we began to guestimate at the number of mice in their garage. Our son informed us that mice have a gestation period of about one month or less and one month is the time it takes for a littler mouse to reach maturity.

So, if there was one expectant female country mouse in a box when our neighbors moved off of the farm and into the city, she would give birth within a month and set the city mouse colony wheels in motion. How many mice might there be within six months?

Let's say each female mouse had an average of ten babies (five females and five males). As was the case in our neighbors garage, there was plenty of food (bags of wheat), housing (boxes storing books and other collectibles) and bedding (boxes of cloth and clothing). These were ideal breeding conditions. Within six months, there could be approximately five hundred mice. Within one year, there could be one hundred thousand mice. And within two years, there could be as many as four billion mice!

Talk about permutations and combinations! We went on to talk about how when the garage was full, the house would be entered. This then led us into a discussion of the value of predators in nature to keep the balance. Get out the mouse traps or send in the cats!

Counting Money

Pocket change thrills little kids: pennies, nickels, dimes, quarters, half dollars and dollars. Bills thrill big kids: ones, fives, tens, twenties, fifties, one hundreds and so on. The kids are in their counting house, counting all their money.

Whether you encourage your kids to save their money or you allow them to spend it, they will be learning math. As they save it, count it, spend it and receive change from it, they will be learning mathematical concepts.

As the little ones sort, pile, stack and examine their coins, they begin to understand the value of each and the relationship between them. One dollar equals two half dollars equals four quarters equals ten dimes equals twenty nickels equals one hundred pennies. These are tough concepts for little kids to understand at first, but if you toss them some change, understand they will.

Money math is a part of life. There is no avoiding it. Knowing how much change is due you is a necessity if you don't want to end up being cheated out of your cash and what better way to learn than to do. As kids use money, they learn how to use it. Whether they spend it, save it or even if they lose some of it, they will learn how to count it. Money matters and money is math.

More Counting

I discovered that by counting by more than just ones and twos for my children, they began to absorb concepts hidden within the multiplication table.

1,2,3,4,5,6,7,8,9,10 . . . 2,4,6,8,10,12,14,16,18,20 . . .
3,6,9,12,15,18,21,24,27,30 . . . 4,8,12,16,20,24,28,32,36,40 . . .
5,10,15,20,25,30,35,40,45,50 . . . 6,12,18,24,30,36,42,48,54,60 . . .
7,14,21,28,35,42,49,56,63,70 . . . 8,16,24,32,40,48,56,64,72,80 . . .
9,18,27,36,45,54,63,72,81,90 . . . 10,20,30,40,50,60,70,80,90,100

Putting out a multiplication table where they could have fun with it, helped them begin to solidify the concepts. I never made them memorize the table. They've been absorbing it instead. It was never something I did in a teaching or schooling way. Just for fun for them and for myself too (I memorized the table way back when but when schools out, you begin to forget what was taught and what you memorized).

Counting comes into play and into every day. Kids count their collections, their treats, their toys and the list goes on. Counting is another natural.

Sciences

Look What the Cat Dragged In

Now that our flea infestation is over and we finally won the war the little suckers declared on us, I can write about our flea adventure. Our family's migration westward brought us to the ocean, the milder moister climate, and a land where vegetation and vermin thrive. As much as I love animal life, I'll admit I'll only tolerate vermin elsewhere. Not in my house!

Despite our attempts to encourage our cat to wear the necessary concoctions to ward off fleas, one day we saw a flea in the house. Where there is one, there are always more. Within a few days we realized we were infested.

At first, the few fleas we found hopping around us were a source of amusement and amazement. Our teenage son commented on the wonder of the creatures: how high and far they could catapult themselves.

One of my brothers suggested we set traps to catch them (a natural approach with no chemicals—I liked the idea): set a spot-light over a large bowl of water at night. There were little fleas floating, swimming or drowning under the water that first morning and many mornings after.

The whole family enjoyed studying the specimens floating on the water firstly and then mostly, on a tray under the microscope. Our admiration of their ability to jump so high for their size was enhanced and explained when we saw the length and structure of their hind legs. It was fun for the whole family to watch them kick and spin, sidelying on the microscope tray in the drop of water.

As our bodies became covered in tremendously itchy bites, that seemed forever itchy and took forever to heal, the thrill of the scientific discovery began to wear thin. We were after a solution. Vacuuming daily didn't do it. This herb and that one didn't do it. This spray and that one didn't quite do it. Finally, we beat the problem, a combination of things, but we were finally flea and flea-bite free (brewers yeast powder, garlic, vinegar, cedar, citronella and a household flea killer spray with residual power).

Throughout the curiosity and curse, many questions begged answers. How can fleas jump so high for their size? Why do they bite us? Why do the bites itch so much for so long? Why don't fleas like cedar and all those herbs? Why do we have to spray the whole house? Why do the fleas like to jump into the light? Why do fleas want to jump into heat? Why and how indeed! Questions need answers. That's science.

Gerbilology

We enjoyed two gerbil sisters for a year until the unfortunate demise of one of them. The kids learned not to put the large flat rock on top of the shavings or gravel instead of the gravel or shavings around the rock. They learned how a small mistake like that can end in death. The little critter had dug herself under the rock and was crushed or suffocated to death.

Within a very short time, the difference between life and death was unmistakable. A dead gerbil just does not look alive. Death is still. Life's cycle inevitably results in death.

After the kids had grieved their little pet, I offered to buy another one. Our favorite pet store had only albinos that day, so my kids chose the spunkiest one. "What's an albino? Why are it's eyes red like that?" I did my best to explain genetics and inbreeding. My teenage son had more answers than I did, because of his years of self-directed home schooling study. A little question from little kids can grow into an afternoon's learning experience.

Our oldest son checked out the gender of the newly chosen gerbil: male. With this discovery came the topic of rodent reproduction, which would become more than theory much sooner than I would have expected.

Three baby gerbils were born on our oldest son's fifteen birthday. The excitement turned to sorrow the following day as we watched the parents neglect them. All three of the newborns had died within twenty-four hours. There were many questions from the littler ones about such a tragedy. Why? Why? Why?

Within a month, there were five more babies. By the second day, only three survived. With a little help from our oldest son (he removed the father temporarily to promote mother/infant bonding) the three lived day-to-day. It became obvious that one of the babies had a slight deformity. More learning opportunities.

That little mother went on to have more babies and each litter had more, with more surviving. Through it all, our oldest son enjoyed breading the genetic tries for certain characteristics. This was a science experiment that gave our little ones many littler ones to love and then we shared our science with others through sales and give-aways.

Mousing Around

Our oldest son discovered our cat one day, mousing around in the neighbors' garage. The cat had uncovered a little nest in a cup and he had made all but two babies disappear. Our son, being a true humanitarian and zoologist, rescued the remaining babies and took them in to introduce them to his female gerbil who had just had her own litter of little pinkies.

Will she accept them or will she kill them? That was the question. Amazingly, she responded with maternal fervor (perhaps she had learned from me). Hustling and bustling about, she carried them into the soft, safe confines of her nest, where they each took turns squirting out. She didn't seem to notice that these two were more mature than her own, nor that they were trying to find their own mamma, nor that they were not her own, nor that her little litter had increased by two.

As the days passed, we all looked in on the little bigger brood. My own little brood had questions, "Can't she tell that the mice are mice, Mommi? How come the mice have bigger ears than the gerbil babies? Why are the mice's legs longer than the gerbils? Why do the mice have pointier faces?"

The more we watched, the more we learned. The more we learned, the more we knew and the more we knew, the more we knew we didn't know. As it happened, the mice eventually escaped out of the cage and the cat found them. That was the end of our mice/gerbil experiment.

Slugs Away

Someone accidentally stepped on a slug in the back yard. It wasn't long before flies were buzzing around the dead little creature and then yellow jackets came in to claim the kill. My three youngest children squatted around to see the insect feast.

"Daddy! Daddy! Come see the bugs on the squished slug." My husband happily happened to be home that day and he became as curious about the goings on as the kids were. Being childlike, in the sense that his curiosity is alive and well, he went in the house and dug out the zoom lens of our camera.

The accidental death of a slug offered an interesting afternoon of scientific study. We all ended up out there, in the back yard, an audience to a common happening in the insect world. Death giving life.

With the zoom lens, my husband could marvel at the relatively enormous chunks of meat that the yellow-jacket carved out to take home for future feasting. The meat-carrying flyer hovered awkwardly back to home-base, loaded down with food supply.

It was all over in a few hours. Amazingly, there was little left. To our surprise, our cat was intensely interested in cleaning off the sidewalk remains, "Hey Mom! The cat likes slugmeat too!" It was another lesson in the balance of nature and how nature takes care of itself.

Learning in Tides

We were snacking at our favorite secluded rocky beach shortly after moving to the west coast. Our youngest daughter found a way to mucky up her sneakers, just before we were about to board our van to drive home.

I asked our oldest son to rinse out the little runners in the ocean and thinking they'd wash back to shore, he tossed the sneakers into the sea. He just assumed the tide was washing in like the last time we were there. The kids all learned that day, that the tide was washing out. Sometimes the tide washes in and sometimes it washes out.

The cycle of the tide, was the lesson of that day. My husband proceeded to do research about the tides. How often and when they changed. Incoming and outgoing, high and low. I didn't pay much attention, but when we want to go for a warm swim at another favorite beach front, a long beach, just after the high tide comes in on the hot sand, it's nice to know my husband has answers. He can tell us when our dip will be ideal.

When you home school naturally, every outing is a learning field trip and every holiday teaches lessons. Learning is life and it is fun.

Science of a Social Kind

The more children learn about the world around them, the more they want to learn. Their genuine interest in other people: cultures, colors and creeds, spurs on their questions and begs for answers.

If I added up the questions my children have asked me about our world: other countries and cultures in the news; people in the past, long ago and far away; and things like why the people of the world wage war on each other; I could wrap a chain of questions around the world. All the questions that they field about the world around us can send us on intellectual field trips around the world.

Back in school, I hated the current and world events lessons and quizzes and tests. I didn't care about what my teacher was trying to teach me, I just tried to cram the facts for the finals. Now I am as interested in what is going on and what has gone on in the world as my kids are. We are learning because we want to know. We're not memorizing in an effort to pass a test. We're studying because we are curious.

Ironically, current events around the world, my most hated and dreaded subject twenty years ago in public school, is now one of our family favorites, especially of our eldest son who is of the age I was when I hated world news.

Role Playing Around

He was just one of those acquaintance friends. Public schooled, from a broken home. Unhappy, rebellious, bored, hanging out. A skater for a year or two. He and the guys and their skateboards. At the mall, after hours he'd invite our teenage son from time to time.

That was just one phase he went through. Anarchy was the next one. Our son started looking for excuses for not associating with this neighbor, "He's getting a little scary, Mom. A lot of drugs, and this anarchy stuff now."

"What's that? Anarchy?"

"Well . . . it's not a religion but a philosophy. There's a bunch of them. They believe in no law. You know, lawlessness. Sort of like the Old West, only worse."

I thought I was the only one worrying about that guy. I'd never really felt comfortable about my son getting together with him. The stuff on his jacket bothered me: Mega Death and such, swastikas, inverted penta-grams and the like. I was relieved when my son just feigned busy-ness when the anarchists would come to call.

Our son got to thinking about what the country would be like if anarchy caught on. That led to a shell of a novel about the future where anarchists have torn apart the country. Soon he was working on a comic book effort based on his story with his cousin and a friend. Later, he began designing a role playing game with another home schooling friend.

Almost daily, these two fifteen-year-old young men worked at their role playing game and planned a campaign that would last for months. A campaign that took them into the future and all across North America at first and then into the rest of the world.

Some of their tactics included the New Democratic Russia (and all before Gorbachev's capture and the coup in the summer of '91 and Yeltsin's declaration of The Commonwealth of Independent States of Russia).

Now and then I would pay attention to their discussions of their exploits (I am wary of the dungeons and dragons call-in-the-demons role playing darkness). As I listened, I realized that this game was an educa-tion in itself. Geography, military maneuvers, strategy, weaponry, logistics, history, anthropology, sociology, accounting, mathematics, and I lost track of the rest of the subjects they covered.

Armed with their atlases, dictionaries, thesauruses and other assorted reference books, these guys delved into the world around them and the possibilities of the future that lies ahead of them. No doubt the game got them thinking deeply. They also learned a great deal more than I could ever assess by listening in. Just learning fun in the summer.

A year later, our son began to research anarchy in-depth. That led to more political and philosophical research. He studied the Libertarian thoughts and ideals. He read up on the history of a multiplicity of political ideologies. The librarians became weary of his frequent visits— they know him well for he visits there often. More yearning and learning in the summer-holiday-land of home schooling.

16. THE ARTS

(Visual Arts, Music, Drama)

Visual Arts

Born Artists

I really believe every child is born an artist. Pablo Picasso said, "Every child is an artist. The problem is how to remain an artist once he grows up." We're not all Pablo Picassos and many of us don't want to be. For every individual artist there is an individual kind of art. That's what I really focus on when I look at the art of others and especially the art of children.

We're not all going to paint like Picasso or Da Vinci or any other famous artist you could name. We couldn't all learn to sculpt like Michelangelo. Every individual will have their own style as well as preferences, their unique abilities and individual potential.

As I have watched little children draw, paint and craft, I have seen developmental similarities among them as well as uniquely individual differences. Some of their exclusive traits demonstrate elements of their personality traits. Other traits are more subtle or elusive.

All children need to develop their potential as artists with materials and tools; elbow room and a little sincere praise doesn't hurt either. To attain craftsman expertise and ability or certain specific skills, a mentor or an example to follow is necessary, but pure original art needs only the chance for expression. Criticism, judgments and other opinionated comparisons tend to be counterproductive.

While little kids can show off their great spontaneously artistic talent with just a pencil and paper, they can create really impressive works with quality paints on canvas boards. (I suggest water cleanable acrylics and inexpensive painting paper practice pads or flat white latex painted massonite board to begin with.)

Silly Putty® and play dough offer temporary molding pleasures while dough art and clay can produce works with lasting joys. When considering arts and crafts products, consider toxicity. Little kids shouldn't be given the chance to nibble on toxic paints and clays. For tiny tots, edible play dough is great for molding and food coloring makes a fine watercolor paint. Try making your own watercolors too, from fruits and vegetables such as berries and beets.

Whatever arts and crafts mediums you offer your children, give them room to create, unbounded by the expected blue-sky/green-grass pictures and clay ashtrays long since commonly cliché in the public schools. I can't believe kids are still bringing home that stuff, but they are. Public schools tend to kill creativity. Natural home schools can nurture it like nothing else.

Art Immersion

One talented couple of artists moved into our neighborhood from Italy (and formerly, Romania). It wasn't long before we became friends. Not long after that, they began to inquire about our home schooling kids. A little longer and they dove in with their three children.

As one who has inherited three hundred years of family tradition in the art world, the mother of these three kids continued sharing her work with them as she never could before. Skilled in silverwork and schooled in architecture, the father of this family was able to share his work with his children as well. When they were beholding to the public school, there wasn't enough time for an apprenticeship. From mother and father to son and daughter, home schooling is apprenticing of a natural kind.

It's always a great feeling to see another family embrace their own home school, and in turn they embrace each other. Their kids are still following in their parents' footsteps. A family of artists. From parents to their children, the art is passed down the generations, instead of the lost art it could have become because of the public schools. Home art school and all the beautiful art within it: it's a beautiful thing to see.

Music

Play it Again, Dad

Music appreciation was the only musical course my husband had taken before I met him. For a guy who couldn't really play or sing a thing, not in perfect pitch or tune anyway, he sure did appreciate a vastly varied array of music. With all my piano lessons and all the other musical experience I had behind me, my music library couldn't hold a candle to his.

I had concentrated on making music while he had expertise in playing it. Our kids will probably always thank him for all the music he's played throughout their growing up. From classical and ethnic to pop and rock and many interesting assortments inbetween and round about, we've all learned to appreciate the banquet of music styles that abound (anything within our good taste, anyway).

As my husband puts on his favorites, our kids fall in love with many of them and the littler they are, the more they seem to say, "Play it again, Dad!" So, he does, again and again, until we grow tired of even our most favorite songs. Our children sing and dance along, memorizing the tunes, the words and rhythms.

Notes, Keys and Instruments

I wonder if listening to so many differing types of good music has given our children more than all the piano lessons I took as a child. The piano teacher taught me to hate the piano. It wasn't until I discovered the piano on my own after several years of boycotting it, that I learned to love to play.

Music and the instruments that play it, is another miracle of the world to our children. They dream of playing like the musicians they listen to. If it is in them, I believe they can, someday. If they want to.

Our teenaged son has taught himself to play the piano, in a very short period of time. No lessons, just a few questions answered from me, when he asked them of me. Not only has our son taught himself to play, but my husband can pick out a few tunes too. They both read music better than some people who have taken years of lessons. A day or two after our son took up the Celtic tin whistle, he was playing surprisingly well.

I am continually amazed at the power of the human mind to teach itself if there is desire and incentive within. At fourteen, our son decided to learn how to read notes and play the piano. Our seven-year-old daughter followed suite. She plays by ear and sight more than by reading notes, but she's learning what she wants to learn and that's what really counts. My sister plays by ear more than I can play by notes and ear combined (she was younger and piano lessons for her were neglected, so she copied those who played around her).

The more instruments you have around, the more children will want to learn to play them. I used to go down into the basement storage room to play the trumpets my dad had packed away. There was an old banged up silver one we were allowed to get out and play and we did often, but the shiny golden brass one was off limits: Dad's pride and joy. I must confess that the urge to play that *good* trumpet was irresistible. We played the special trumpet more than the bumpety trumpety that was considered ours (Shhh! Don't tell my father!).

Playing good quality music provides excellent mentors. Videos of musicians performing their craft offer even more of an example for children to follow. Our youngest is wild about old musicals: movies on video, that she watches regularly, repeatedly and memorizes songs and dances. If children grow up around people who play, they'll want to follow in their musical footsteps. Having my brother's band over to practice gave me a beating desire to play drums and guitars. Making music a part of life is the key.

The Piano Tuner Came

Just an old upright piano. A steal of a deal at an auction. It sounded horrible the day the movers brought it: klinkity klink, klinkity klunk. I didn't know if the piano tuner could help the old thing out of it's misery.

He was a musical caricature. Short, sort of skinny, with balding long wavy, slightly messy hair hanging over his slightly hunching shoulders and wisping around his granny glasses. The dog didn't especially like him any more than the little kids did. She bared her fangs, coupled with intermittent growls and barking. They hid nearby.

Mr. Music went to work on the old keyboard box, playing a few tunes in-between careful plunketing. He made the old piano sound so good, I applauded.

It wasn't long before my children were gathered round, asking Mr. Piano Tuner questions about what he was doing. His genteel manner befriended them quickly and I think he enjoyed their interest and help as much as they enjoyed the piano tuning lesson.

That simple piano tuning task turned out to be a most memorable afternoon for our children. They learned about pitch and tone and saw the connection between the keys, hammers and wires (strings). For seven, six and four year olds, the miracle of music from the piano was a most amazing happening.

For days and weeks afterward, they had to climb up to look in at the hammers and wires, crawl under to look at the connections to the keys and just pursue all-around inspections of this world of wonder within the world. The piano will never look or sound the same to them, again.

Drama

Don't Worry, It's Just Pretend

"Mommi! Mommi! My leg is bleeding!" She screamed and wailed, sending horrifying pains up and down my spine and down my legs. Jolting out of my writing chair, I ran to salvage my little one from disaster, only to find my younger three in the midst of a somebody-got-hurt game.

They'll either fill my head with gray hair or stop my heart for good one of these days. I've lost count of all the many times my children have scared the stuffing out of me. Not crying wolf, just acting.

When they play, I call it dramatization. Of course, they act out plenty of peaceful plays. They've been dogs, cats and horses for days on end. They've been mommies and daddies and birdies too. They get into their part and the part gets into them. Kids can act like nobody's business.

They act so convincingly that if they wanted to pursue careers in acting, they could succeed. Like all other children, they were born to act, to dramatize, to pretend. The only reason children wouldn't perform well in an audition is that their performances are spontaneous and somewhat private.

Sometimes, when they are lost in their world of drama and I enter the room, the action stops: quiet on the set, somebody big is watching us. If they are playing out a scene around or under my feet, the show goes on as long as they don't know I'm watching.

Self-consciousness usually grows as they grow older. If children can get over the worry of being watched, they could keep their natural acting abilities into adulthood. I tend to think that's what makes some actors great at their craft: they can keep or get back their childhood intensity or focus on playing a part.

Children don't need acting or dramatic lessons. Adults do. Adults could learn a thing or two about acting by watching children for a while, as long as the kids don't become aware of being watched. A child's world is full of pretending. Pretending is acting. Acting is drama is pretending.

Just for fun, we let our kids try some extra work in the movie and television business. It was a great learning experience and we used the money for learning allowances. The greatest thing I think the kids learned was how fake the Hollywood way is: fake dirt, fake blood, fake beauty, fake love, fake audiences, fake everything. They've never looked at the movies quite the same since. Now they know that what they see on the screen is often pretend. Now they've added another game to their repertoire: Quiet on the set! Action!

17. ATHLETICS

(Sports, Dance, Play)

Sports

Fun and Games

The thrill of winning, the agony of defeat, healthy competition, constructive criticism. These are things most little kids could do without. Being too busy to teach my kids much in the way of games, I've been delighted to witness the way they have immersed themselves in fun creating their own games; a new game every hour, a new way every day.

Young children don't tend to be good losers, nor do they go after more competition than they already have dumped in their laps. As they grow older, their need to compete may grow and their ability to lose with dignity and win with grace will also grow. All these things in due time and each according to his or her ability. Our eldest has come to crave plenty of healthy competition. The younger ones are starting to enjoy a little competition here and there as well.

After careful and lengthy observation, I really think little kids would rather have fun and games without competition and referees. There will be rules to be sure, usually flexible and ever changing, evolving to fit the situation; but the kids like to make their own rules, together.

Having grown up swimming upstream in competition, I'm happy to let my kids play games, invent them, create them, agreeing on the rules, altering them when they feel the need. It's fun for me to see what is born and it's fun for them, and all the while they are getting exercise (sometimes quite intense workouts), attaining agility and ability and learning (to create and cooperate). It's just the beginning of learning the fun and games of life.

Competition

If children begin to want competition, they will seek it out. I do believe in competition, but not coerced upon little kids nor forced upon those older gentler ones who would just as soon do without it. Too much competition when young may scare kids out of competing at all: the fear of failure may set in. If children grow into competition, at their own speed and in their own time, they may learn to love it as they learn about it. Some of mine have, naturally.

As children grow older, they create more competition for themselves. Our eldest son has been involved in street hockey, freelance football, and various types of baseball with his friends over the past years. Plenty of competition abounds amidst the redefined rules and referee-free freelance games they put together according to need and available players.

As much as I had steered him away from competitive organized sports, our teen son wanted to jump into football or baseball at a nearby public high school. I was surprised to discover that none of the high schools in our area offered after-school sports! Thus were my worries about football injuries relieved, to our son's dismay and disappointment. The little he wanted from the public school, they didn't even deliver anymore.

At any age, kids can jump into the competition and start competing. Many late starters have jumped in and jumped up to the top. From gymnastics to skating to hockey to swimming to tennis to weightlifting to skiing and so on, many have gone into a sport late by competitive comparison, caught up and passed.

Competition need not start young. In most cases it shouldn't be imposed and it definitely should not be forced upon little children. Too much competition isn't natural. Until kids get old enough to crave more of it, competition should remain limited to competition for toys, parental attention and all those other things children naturally fight to win.

Chores

Speaking of competition and games: these things have been incorporated into the household work and chores around our house, not so much at my instigation, but because of my children's implementation. They often make a game or a contest out of cleaning up their room and other various areas of our house.

We also often play music to make cleaning up a more pleasant experience. Unfortunately, we often end up dancing. Consequently, our house isn't as clean as it used to be nor as it could be, but it's a happy home. Who'd rather clean than dance anyway? I confess, I give into my cleanliness impulses and get the house clean regularly. I can only dance so long midst a mess. We often clean and then we dance.

Dance

Let's Dance

Choreography aside, natural free-style dance, front and center. Just play music for children and they'll choreograph their own steps, sways and spins. I love to watch little kids groove to music. They are so free, so creative and so natural. Natural dancers: I think all children are.

My husband and I have been family dancing with our kids since the beginning of our times together. I have gradually left all my trained and professional dance steps behind in favor of natural dancing for fun. We don't dance to be seen or applauded by others. We dance for ourselves. And while we dance, we exercise our way to physical health, coordination comes without concentrating and the rhythm gets us going. Dancing is a natural.

Of course there are those who want the choreographed way and that's another choice. Another natural. It is natural to want order. There are different types and degrees of order. Every one and every family has the natural right to decide what dance they will dance.

As my girls have been getting older, they have begun to show interest in such dancing as tap and highland, where they want to copy steps. No interest in lessons, yet, but they like to copy what they see on video. I don't push them along, but I'm supportive as they yearn to learn some steps. Sometimes we like to learn a predetermined dance, but most of the time, free dance wins in our house. I love to see the results of the interpretive dance of children.

Play

Tickle Me, Chase Me

Both arms up, my little four year old daughter says, "Here's my armpits, Mommi! Tickle me, he, hee, heeeee!" Infectious laughter rings throughout the house as I grant her request. Laughter, that best of medicines, is also exercise, a toxin cleanser and a pain killer. Tickle-time is one of her playtime favorites. She has many more.

"Chase me! Chase me! Come and get me! Come and find me! Where am I?" And the list of chase-me find-me playtime favorites could go on. Children can really work up a sweat and pittery pattery heart-beats chasing each other around.

Throughout all the play from day to day, children often incorporate from simple fluid-movement exercises to amazingly extensive acrobatics. Their spontaneous and natural play seems to exercise every little muscle in their bodies.

If children playing doesn't incorporate athletics and aerobics, I don't know what does. From their deep squats to their expansive stretches to their twists and twirls, kids are little athletic wonders. (Their naturally tendency towards athletics is what spurs some adults on to exploit some of them in gymnastics, for example.) Look at little kids for a little while. Can you do what they can do?

Unfortunately in the public schools, energetic kids are forced to sit out their days in desks. Too many hours, days, weeks, months and years go by; and then they have forgotten how to use their bodies. Little children should have the right to use their bodies naturally, to play much of their day away.

Those schools which have allowed children to play half of their day, have better academic results. Kids who study all day don't do as well as children who play as many hours as they study. A fit body sharpens the mind. The creativity exercise that play offers also increases the intellect. Good scientists play towards great discoveries.

Let them play and they will play plenty. The play will be good for them body, mind and soul. Kids were born to play, to learn through play, to exercise through play, to work through play. Play is a full-time job to a kid. The smaller they are, the more they should be school-free to play most of the day. The more we play when we grow out of play as we grow older, the healthier we will be too. Don't forget to play.

Gun Control

Cops and Robbers, Cowboys and Indians, GI Joes—just the beginning of the games we used to play—just part of growing up. A generation later, our eldest flew into Star Wars, jumped into GI Joes and then joined his many friends in daily neighborhood wargames. Neither my husband nor I liked guns at all, not to mention seeing our son play guns with his friends day in and day out. We never bought him guns, but he used sticks and his hand complete with pointer finger until his friends made sure he rose above the underprivileged gunless class, when his birthday came around.

I tried to encourage games of exploration, treasure hunts and anything I could think of to get him and his friends playing creative games that did not include war. Hunting for treasure would result in a war over the find. Exploration games would end up in fights over territory. It was all in fun and even I had to admit there was a great deal of creativity involved in all the strategic warfare and military maneuvering.

I must add that my husband's small passion against guns had everything to do with the fact that his father had numerous bullet holes in his body, his souvenirs of the second world war. My bad feelings towards guns probably came from having had a friend who lost an eye during drunken gun play. We both were against violence.

There came a point in our parenting when we outlawed guns forevermore in our home. We kept our sons away from friends who could play nothing but war-games, for a time. Ending the warring was an endless battle. We lost.

Eventually, I read an article about guns and kids and wargames, and I admit, it began to change my mind on that one. I came away reconsidering the whole warplay thing. After much consideration, I concluded (risking unpopularity with many other parents who oppose wargaming), that if children play war, they might just need to.

Maybe they need to fight out their fears about it. Perhaps they need to work out some aggression. Like in dreams where they can conquer all, children need play for the same reasons. When war is all around us, is it fair to demand that our children not work through their questions, concerns and fears through playing wargames?

It seems to be a natural need for many children. More for some, less for others. My younger three children have had less to do with playing war than my first. We can only imagine why they need to play some of the games they choose.

As parents in our home, we decided to concentrate our fight against violence and peer dependence syndrome (which can translate into gang activities) instead of against guns. We won that one.

Guns are not the bad guys. Real guns can be dangerous and must be respected, like so many other powerful forces, cars and fires, to name two. I grew up around cars and trucks, campfires and bonfires, and guns and rifles. I respected all aforementioned. As far as guns go, it would be far better for children to learn realities about guns with and through their parents than on the streets or school grounds. In the many years since we fought and lost our big fight against toy guns, we have given in here and there, not to violence, but to guns.

Here's a funny story another home schooling mother told me. Her formerly genteel son suddenly became interested in guns for no apparent reason (most of his friends were from *no guns* families as he was). They finally agreed to allow him a little toy gun. When a friend came over and discovered the gun, the friend promptly beat him up for harboring a weapon. When the friend's mother was told, she said, "Well, he shouldn't have had a gun in the first place." The mindset of this other family was that guns were bad but violence was not. Excuse me?

I know a man who gets almost violently angry about people who want to keep the right to own guns. His anger is palpable. When I really begin to think about that, it confuses me. Why does he see red because my grandfather kept a large rack of guns in his basement? All those guns and all those years and no one was ever hurt by them. His car almost killed him and my grandmother twice and in the end a truck took my grandmother's life. We've had too many discussions about all the reasons pro and con for gun control. In the end I always come back to believing in personal freedoms.

After many years of consideration (not to mention research), I have come to a belief that the right to bear arms, or more directly, the right to protect oneself and one's family, is a fundamental one that seems to have far reaching repercussions. Where people maintain the right to protect themselves, politicians and criminals dare encroach only so far. Taking guns away from law abiding citizens creates a void that begs to be filled and the state will fill it to the degradation of freedom.

There are parents who do not allow toy guns of any type, but they always seem to make exceptions for water guns including super duper soakers. Hypocritically humorous. At least I was consistent: I only allowed plant sprayers when guns were outlawed in our home. Or was I? Who knows.

Go with your feelings on this one, but you might be going against good nature if you say no to guns in your home and yard. There is such a thing as repressed anger and rage. What if toy guns are a healthy way for kids to release their anger and tension? Who knows? Who knows, indeed.

18. OTHER A'S

Assimilation

A natural alternative to the tedious rote memorization methods that are so much a part of the public school experience is assimilation, which comes naturally. We are always assimilating information whether we recognize it or not, much like the way we assimilate nutrients from the foods we eat.

Ironically, it seems that those bits of information we most easily and unknowingly absorb, are those that stay with us the longest. What we try so hard to memorize often escapes us sooner than that which came to us so easily. It isn't so much that what we memorize is toughest to remember, but that the harder we try, the harder it seems to be to learn in a lasting way.

When learning happens naturally as assimilated information during an experience in life, it seems to stick. David P. Gardner explains, "We learn simply by the exposure of living. Much that passes for education is not education at all but ritual. The fact is that we are being educated when we know it least."

To gain knowledge and wisdom, it must be found by the individual. Marcel Proust said, "We don't receive wisdom; we must discover it for ourselves after a journey that no one can take for us or spare us."

As Aristotle once said, "What we have to learn to do, we learn by doing." And by doing we learn. Live and learn. As we live, we assimilate, we learn. Assimilating is natural learning.

Constantly and consistently I am amazed as I watch my children assimilate information both small and grand, day after day, week upon week, month to month and throughout the years we've been traveling on this natural learning quest.

One son assimilated cursive writing along the way: I don't know when or where he picked it up exactly (he said he read little notes over my shoulder). Another son assimilated phonics and carefully sounded out word by word on the learning to read path while another daughter preferred assimilating whole words, word by word. I'd have to say most of what our children have learned (even our walking encyclopedia teen), was assimilated along the way. They haven't really been *taught* much at all. Sometimes I hate to admit how little I've taught them. What I have taught, I have taught mostly by example. What wasn't example, was guidance and encouragement.

Children learn to walk and talk by association and assimilation. Thus begins their natural learning adventure.

Assessment

When *to test or not to test* is the question, assessment is the only natural answer. Tests might be what a teacher of thirty students needs to figure out who might know what, and who gets to pass to the next grade, but home schooling parents don't need a test to know how well their children are doing.

Barnaby C. Keeney has commented, "At college age, you can tell who is best at taking tests and going to school, but you can't tell who the best people are. That worries the hell out of me." His thoughts stare in the face of the public school system and all the tests. What are all those tests for?

Eugene S. Wilson once said, "Only the curious will learn and only the resolute overcome the obstacles to learning. The quest quotient has always excited me more than the intelligence quotient." He isn't the only one questioning the IQ test after all these years of the masses being labeled by them.

Even though the IQ test is in question in some circles, just for fun, at the request of our eldest son a couple of years ago, we each took it. To our amazement, we all did well. Incidentally, our highest score came from one of our youngest family members. When I tell some anti-home schooling people that our children are gifted and therefore school at home, they tend to leave us alone. I recommend such explanations. Tell people your kids are autistic savants if you have to!

Just as "A man is not idle because he is absorbed in thought. There is a visible labor and there is an invisible labor," as Victor Hugo once said; tests cannot really tell us what knowledge resides inside a child. As children resist being taught they also resist being tested. Tests are an insult to their intelligence.

There are many things children know that they can't or won't show they know on a test or in a testing situation. I have long since learned that healthy, happy, self-esteemed kids really object to having tests imposed upon them. It's fundamentally insulting and patronizingly condescending to test someone, child or adult. None of us really like it.

While some tests are necessary, particularly at higher levels of learning, skill and expertise, as in a medical doctor; most tests kids grow up with are counterproductive and contrary to the learning process. Most importantly, tests don't tell us much at all, except, perhaps, who has persistent memory.

One key difference between a pass and a fail is memory retention. Those who pass tests remember the required information long enough to get the grade. I often did well on school tests, but as soon as the test was passed, I would forget the information I had crammed into my memory. Since what we don't use, we lose, what kids cram for tests, they often forget.

While we, as people who are or should always be learning something, often do forget those things that were imposed upon us, as teachings in public schools; we remember best those things we searched after ourselves. The natural learning process begets things remembered longer than those things force fed and soon forgotten.

Our own natural home school has just produced it's first graduate: our first son, who at mid-seventeen, decided on his own to take his GED exams early in 1994. He ranked in the top 85 percent to 95 percent in the U.S., in four out of the five subject areas. All this was accomplished with minimal exam preparation after ten years of self-directed study, part of the natural learning process. Thus the result of his first tests in ten years!

For those who need to know how well their kids are doing, quietly assessing progress from the sidelines of learning is the best bet. Don't impose tests when they are avoidable. Just assess the situation. Glance in on them from time to time. The more we stay out of our childrens' business of learning, the more they seem to learn. The less we test them, the more they trust us. Just assess their progress from the sidelines as you are cheering them on.

Associations

Family relations are excellent exercises in the art of friendship. Home is the place we practice socializing for the first time. Socialization: there's that word again. The fundamental societal unit is the family. If the family breaks down, society breaks down. If children have a healthy, happy, stable social order in their home, they are being properly socialized into society.

I consider associating another A of learning. Associating, more commonly known as socialization, seems to be the most popular educational fundamental. It's the one thing I get flack for, for home schooling our kids. The nosy trouble-making neighbor type will always look for what must be socially wrong with our kids because they are home schooling.

While few question that our kids are learning, some are quick to point out that maybe our kids won't be like everybody else's kids because they aren't standing in line, putting up their hands, waiting their long-awaited turns and on and on down there at the public school.

No. Home schooled kids aren't usually just like public schooled kids. They are usually more mature, more polite, more considerate, more happy, more confident and more many good things. They have been naturally socialized and if they have good and decent parents, they will be learning to be good and decent children. That is the rule, rather than the exception from what I've seen.

Unfortunately, home schooled kids can and do fit in quite well sometimes. They are often all too normal. Sometimes they fight, sometimes they cuss, sometimes they do those naughty things that ordinary children do. Even kids from exceptionally good families sometimes go awry somewhat. Perhaps if children were completely removed from the bad, that is within our society, they wouldn't be so normal. Yes, home-schooled children are often all too normal, but they usually are noticeably more well-adjusted.

Most of all, most of us home schoolers are good friends within our families. Parents and children: close friendships. Close family ties. Our home schooling attitude is that family is first. The first place to make friends. The place to practice being pals. And as fewer associations means deeper associations, we prefer to spend more time making a few good friends and less time making many acquaintances. Our favorite associations are within our family.

Attitudes and Altitudes

Self-concept, self-esteem: buzz words the public schools like to use in promoting their little programs to help children like themselves. Unfortunately, the very structure of the public school tends to belittle the esteems of little children.

By happy experience and observation, keeping a child in a happy home is plenty program. Children, given half a chance, will like themselves. Parents who love their children will have children who love themselves and those around them. It's that simple.

Home schooling kids have all the opportunity they need to have healthy self-esteems. The public school's own standard test of social adjustment, the Piers-Harris Children's Self-Concept Scale, has found home schooling kids at the top.

A low self-esteem can keep kids from progressing in all aspects of their lives. As Henry C. Link has said, "While one person hesitates because he feels inferior, the other is busy making mistakes and becoming superior." Feeling free to explore and being confident enough to try is crucial to learning and improving. A healthy self-attitude is crucial to self-direction.

What direction one is headed will lead to one altitude or another. Lower altitudes aren't as lofty as higher ones. While your attitude is crucial to what direction you are headed, your altitude is where you are now. If you have a good attitude you can work towards a higher altitude in life.

Public schools seem to foster the lowest common denominators or lower altitudes. Home schools have the opportunity to raise altitudes higher and many do.

Apprenticeship

Theory is one thing. Practice is everything. Theory can only go so far. Theory is books and formulas and beliefs and ideas and hopes and dreams. Theory must be put into practice in order to be validated. Practice makes perfect. Practical experience goes as it grows. Practice naturally helps the practitioner grow upward towards perfection.

Educational programs that are theoretical in bulk are often not worth the paper they are written on, nor the papers the passer receives. Learning programs that are apprenticeship in nature, are usually worth more because the apprentice has learned practical experience and knowledge which is worth more than theoretical knowledge.

Many home schooling families incorporate one apprenticeship program or another. Of course all mothers and fathers are automatically apprenticing their children in an adult, marriage, parenting and family program. Any skills either parent has and uses around and with their children, such as hobbies and chores, is added to the program.

Any home schooling parents who enjoy the challenge and autonomy of a family or home business (and many do), also usually enjoy incorporating their children into their corporation, company, partnership or proprietorship. Viola! Instant apprenticeship.

Whether or not parents work at or from home, they should try to include their children in the world of what they do for a living as often and as much as possible. Home schooling families have more opportunity to do that, but other families can do it as well. We learn to do things best, watching others do and then doing those things ourselves.

As a computer programmer, networker, maintenance man; my husband has included our four kids in his work so much so that they all are well acquainted with and even immersed in his computer world. As an artist, writer, and designer; I have raised my children around my work and done my work around my children. This is the natural way to make a living and apprenticeship is a natural.

Afterwards

Many people otherwise interested in natural home schooling for their children often worry about life for their children afterwards. What happens after they are eighteen? How do they get their high school diploma? What about college and university? What about a career? Sure, apprenticeship works for a few and there are those who can make great money in sales or in their own business without even a high school diploma, but what about the rest of us who need those little pieces of paper to get anywhere in this complicated world?

Beyond home schooling, a student's life can get on the regular education track quite easily. I have seen home schooled kids go straight into college without ever having taken an exam, when counselors are eager to try out such unique students by letting these kids try a semester or two or three to see how they do. Sometimes the home schooled student is asked to take an entrance exam first or they take their GED exams which is usually considered high school equivalency. Rarely would a student need to actually get their high school diploma, but that isn't such an obstacle even if it is demanded in some cases. There are crash courses that produce high school diplomas in a matter of months in many cases.

Just think about what an immigrant would have to do to get into college. There are ways. A high school diploma is not a necessity. Imagine an eccentric family, traveling the globe while their children grow up (I've met a few myself). What do their children do when college time rolls around? They take entrance exams or they get some exceptions to the rules pulled out for them. There are many ways to get on the college track.

Plenty of home-schooled kids have entered college or university with no more than GED and SAT scores. Some have gone after and received scholarships, even to prestigious universities: Harvard, Yale, Princeton, Stanford. The Colfax brothers are a case in point. One after another, Grant, Drew and Reed Colfax graduated from their home school based on a goat farm to Harvard with math or science scholarships earned, based on their high SAT scores. These young fellows studied by kerosine lamplight at night after a long day of farmwork in Northern California. Schoolwork was their fun at the end of the day (Read David and Micki Colfax's *Home Schooling For Excellence* for details).

There truly is much educational life beyond even natural independent home schooling. The many options are out there waiting to be discovered. You can help your children when the time comes, but chances are they will be better at finding the answers than you will be. That's what self-directed natural home schooling seems to do for your kids.

19. LEARNING

Learning is a fact of nature; a big part of the natural order of things. Learning is and has been life since life began. Children and adults alike learn as their curiosity drives them to observe and to seek out answers. First you yearn and then you learn. Whether people are mildly interested in something, or they have a pressing need, they are driven to learn. It is part of being human and even just a creature of this earth. Yearning is natural. Yearning begets learning.

Much like breathing, learning comes naturally. Especially the basics. Kids can't help themselves. If there are learning opportunities around children, they will breath them in. Set a table full of fruits or display a platter of vegetables before children and they will want to try eating some of them. Likewise, make books, pencils, papers, crayons, paints, clay, scissors, tape and other learning supplies available to kids and they will make good use of them.

When your children play, worry not that they are not learning. Play is learning and learning happens through play. Playing with ideas, inventors innovate. Playing with numbers, mathematicians formulate and so on. Think of your children as junior scientists of sorts because that's what they really are. There is much we can learn from our children about learning itself. They are born masters at it. Many adults have often forgotten how to learn and need lessons from children who could teach them how to play again.

Many parents who consider home schooling their children get concerned about their kids missing out on some subjects because they are missing school. Some parents worry about their children being behind in some areas. I've tended to leave it to my kids to go at their own pace.

As wonderfully easy-going as my husband has been about our kids' home schooling, there were a few times when he worried just a little that they were playing too much, not getting enough math and maybe not reading or spelling up to their age levels, to put it all in a nutshell.

I always assured and reassured him that nature would take it's course. They would learn what they needed to know when they needed it. So far, nature's self-instruction method is working wonderfully for our children. They have been proving themselves up to par and beyond. Yes, they play much of the time, but if you observe them with an open mind, you will see how they are always learning something. That's what they were born to do. They can't help themselves. They are always learning something.

Even when they are plopped in front of the TV they are learning something, bad or good. There were a few years when I had it in for TV. The old one we had blew up one day and I was happy we couldn't afford to get another one. We lived in the current cultural dark for two years. At the height of the Cosby show's early popularity, we had no idea what it was about until we visited relatives one night when it was on. And Family Ties? It's a show?

When we were given a twenty-five dollar auction-deal TV as a gift from a family who took pity on such TV-less poverty, we tasted TV again, discovering many worthwhile learning shows. At first I said no to anything uneducational, but then I began to see there was more to learn than what we see as education. While there is plenty of pulp and garbage on TV, there is still much that is worth enjoying and learning from.

Because of television's power to hypnotize and instruct for the good or for the bad, I have always kept a leash on it. My kids grew up knowing that TV was one of the things they had to ask permission for. No one ever just goes up to it and turns it on (except Daddy, to my dismay!). Our kids can't just watch it. For the most part, they don't want to. There must be a purpose. There must be a moral to the story. We try to control it's power and use it for good.

One of the tools to harnessing the power of television is the video cassette recorder. The VCR can capture shows for later digestion, negating many problems we once contended with: the revolving around the TV time-frame and debates over shows with conflicting time slots are two key examples. Many shows are worth reviewing or keeping for years as well.

While we purchased our VCR with TV control in mind, it has evolved into our time machine. It frequently takes us to places we would otherwise not go, through movies old and new. Our children have enjoyed a rich diet of culture and learning through musicals, classics, wildlife and foreign films (carefully chosen) and some of the vast array of contemporary films available.

Public schools have incorporated television into their classrooms a little more each year to the point that now some schools have something set up that includes commercials to pay for the television programming system they utilize. Some parents in these areas are upset about this and understandably so. We have a "mute the commercial" rule in our home.

Only the most interesting, informative or amusing commercials get "shown" in our home. All our children have become excellent editors. They know how to cut out crap, as we call it.

When our children saw a special news piece on TV in schools, they were stunned and amazed, "Why do kids go to school to watch TV when they can watch those kinds of shows on TV at home? Why don't the schools just send the kids home to watch TV? I think the government should just put the learning shows on TV and let the kids stay home to watch." Why not? Some futurists surmise that such just may be the case in the future. I hope so.

If you have a computer in the house, chances are more likely than not that your children are diving at it. There's something about that mystical mesmerizing monitor. TV's, video games and computers all draw kids or kids at heart to their transfixing monitors (Maybe it also has something to do with that hypnotic electronic hum only some of us can truly hear). Like bees to pollen, kids are drawn to computers, whatever the reasons.

As man-made as computers are, they certainly seem to be a natural. I find them ideal for the natural-learning home school. Not every home schooling parent who has chosen the natural learning path for their children would agree with me, though. I've had a few lively discussions on that matter. Some pro-naturals contend that the computer is a wholly unnatural device that belongeth not in the natural home school, perhaps mostly because they fear that it removes the user too far from life as we know it. Virtual reality is disdained by them.

There are many who feel ill at ease at the thought of so much life being revolved around a machine like the computer. They may imagine nerd upon weird nerd at their screens, taking part in society from a distance, distancing themselves from it; at society's peril. I see the computer as a learning tool and modems as communication tools. Sophisticated tools, no doubt, but that's what makes them so very useful and versatile.

People converse, debate, share and meet over modems, or bulletin board services (BBS's) to be more precise. Couples have met, become friends and subsequently married, not through computer dating services (as so many may have imagined they would), but over computer BBS's.

We have used the computer in our home (thanks so much to my husband) for at least seven of our over ten years home schooling. Our CD–ROM equipped computer has been our electronic typewriter, our never-ending drawing pad, our reading enhancement tool, our spelling and grammar tutor, our dictionary and thesaurus, our graphics design utility, our game device, our shelves of books including more than one encyclopedia set, at least one of our filing cabinets, many of our story books, our pen pal connector, and our window to the world.

Tending towards right brain activity, my inclination was not towards computers, but I willingly went along with sacrificing many other possessions to make way for our ever evolving computer system, in order that our family could take advantage of this technology. Our home school has focused on computer literacy and the natural learning process has only been enhanced by this. No matter what tools we utilize in our home school, I believe we can be in keeping with the spirit of the natural learning laws.

Public schools incorporate computers into their curriculums to be sure, but I've heard too many stories from such kids of them standing in line and waiting their turns, to be convinced there is much computer opportunity there. More and more home schools can take advantage of the versatile computer tool, since each year that goes by computers become more and more affordable as they become more and more powerful (which I have mixed feelings about, incidentally, since we jumped on the computer bandwagon when so much bought so little compared to today's standards).

Money seems often at issue with the public school people. They are always asking for more. If you took a look at the numbers, you would find that numerous big and little private schools manage their money well, producing far better results with far fewer dollars per student, while the big money-sucking public schools demand ever more.

From what I have seen, one key seems to be administration, or administrators to be more precise. The public school machine is so well oiled with administrators, they're dripping. On average, there is one administrator per two hundred and fifty children, while one administrator per three thousand, seven hundred and fifty children is sufficient for the Catholic school system. Small private schools and home schools do better.

Money does not equal learning, even though those teachers on strike and politicians on the take (more tax dollars in this case) keep misleading people towards the notion that it does. In 1990, it cost 300 percent more for education than in 1960 but the results are certainly not 300 percent better! Countless little private schools and home schools do better on bare bones budgets. Why is that? Because they have to! It's a matter of necessity. Give me more money for my home school and I would use it. I could always use more. That doesn't mean that I need more to get satisfactory results, though.

Many who choose home school do so because it is the only private school they can afford. The vast majority of home schooling families are lacking in money, so much so that many of us have learned to transport our schools from home to the library on a monthly, weekly or even sometimes a daily basis. "All you need is love and a library card" is a common saying amongst home schoolers simply because it has had to be so for so many of us. Learning needn't be expensive when it can be free.

There are many ways to learn and many meanings of the words learn/ing, educa/tion and school/ing. Just for fun, check the dictionary to enlighten yourself with descriptions.

The public school as we've known it is simply an institution set up by man and womankind. Schools primarily teach, instruct and pigeon hole children into doing and thinking as those who set up the school curriculum wish them to. It may be accidental and/or calculated that schools seem to try to train children to be students of the state. In some countries, calculated efforts are made to train up the children the way those in power of the state want them to go. Sometimes it's just well-meaning but misguided educators and legislators.

To school does not mean to learn whether or not a dictionary would tell us that. Learning takes place because of nature's or God's design. Natural learning happens because it is necessary to the individual's survival, happiness or to satisfy other needs. As Winston Churchill once said, "I am always ready to learn, although I do not like being taught." My sentiments exactly.

20. TEACHING

Force Feeding

"Eat your peas!" her shrill voice was out of control now.

"But Mom? I try but I can't swallow them. I always gag on them!" I feared I was courting death by challenging her Matriarchal authority, but I couldn't swallow peas if I wanted to. I didn't want this stress nor the punishment coming.

It was their way. The parents of that day. "Clean your plate . . . eat your peas or go to bed without supper." How many baby boomers like me went to bed without supper and/or with a beating simply because they couldn't physically swallow one particular type of food out of all others? How many kids were in big trouble, of the physical kind, because they couldn't remember the stuff their teachers fed them long enough to get the grade their parents wanted them to get? How many kids suffer such unfair punishments today?

School's favorite educational foods are force fed to kids as a matter of course. It's the public school way. The menu is planned, the food is prepared, and the schooling schedule is usually strictly adhered to.

It doesn't seem to matter if the kids aren't hungry for what is being served that day or hour or minute. It doesn't matter if the children are ravenously hungry for something else. What the teacher has to feed the children has to be fed to them. The material must be covered. The course must be finished. Whether or not learning has happened seems to be worse than secondary. What is on the spoon seems to be what matters to the public school.

Some home schools start out spoon feeding and force feeding. Most of us find or figure out that what goes in will come out, but if something is searched for and desired, it will be treasured when found.

Buffet Style

Take hungry children to a buffet style dinner and they will eat. It is inevitable. They will eat something. Maybe just cherry tomatoes, cucumber slices and ice cream. Maybe just mashed potatoes, gravy, roast beast and chocolate milk. The same child will likely eat a few things one time and other things the next.

The nature of growing children includes in large part: hunger. They hunger after food and they hunger after knowledge. They hunger after particular things at particular times. While a child can absolutely crave tomatoes one week, the same child may gag at the thought of tomatoes the next week.

This roller-coaster of needs and wants is the nature of children, "Mommi, Mommi, I want mashed potatoes . . . more . . . more . . . more . . . no Mom, no, I hate potatoes now."

Children seem to crave one thing and binge on it until they're sick of it. They crave and binge, crave and binge, crave and binge, from one thing to another and another and another.

It can drive you crazy if you don't go with the flow. Controlling children against their natural wants and needs is like canoeing upstream. Going with the flow, working with the natural tendencies of children instead of against them, is like cultivating dandelions. Working with nature will help both you and your kids. Controlling can be abusing.

If a child gags at the smell of a certain food, chances are, that food is not what the child needs at the moment. Maybe later. There are other foods the child can benefit from. It is the nature of the human body to crave after the things it needs (Although we will crave things that are bad for us, if we look at what our bodies are trying to tell us, we'll find what they really want. If you crave a naughty salty, maybe your body just wants more sodium, potassium or magnesium rich foods. Kids who crave dirt need more vitamin D, for example).

Learning is like food for kids. They crave answers to their questions. Their seemingly endless energy propels them towards those things they just havta gotta know. Surround them with books and other learning tools and they'll feed themselves, with your asked-for help from time to time.

Parent Teacher Guiding

Parents are the best teaching guides for their children and children are their own best teachers. If we let children learn as they grow in nature's way, they will attain true intelligence of heights they would have never known otherwise. Guide them as in all other aspects of their lives.

Teach them by answering their questions as they ask, and show and share of your knowledge as you feel the needs arise.

Sway towards the thoughts of Harry S. Truman when he said, "I have found that the best way to give advice to your children is to find out what they want and then to advise them to do it."

The best way to be a teaching guide to your children is to be there for them. Be available, be a friend. Be helpful when they ask for your help. Answer their questions. Show them where to look when they ask for reference sources. Don't quiz or test them. Don't criticize or compare them. Always remember and never forget, you are there to help them: a guide to help them in their learning and in their life. Praise and commend.

I like what Charles Schwab had to say about criticism and praise, "Criticism is dangerous, because it wounds (our) pride, hurts (our) sense of importance, and arouses (our) resentment.

"Any fool can criticize, condemn, and complain—and most fools do. I consider my ability to arouse enthusiasm among (others) the greatest asset I possess, that the way to develop the best that is in a (person) is by appreciation and encouragement.

"There is nothing else that so kills the ambitions of a (person) as criticisms from his superiors. I never criticize anyone. I believe in giving (people) incentive to work, so I am anxious to praise but loath to find fault. If I like anything, I am hearty in my approbation and lavish in my praise."

When you see yourself or your children failing, remember what Henry Ford said, "Failure is only the opportunity to intelligently begin again."

Natural failure begs for another beginning. When tiny children fail they try again, automatically. No one need tell them, "If at first you don't succeed, try, try again." When a child falls, he gets up and tries to walk or run again. Try, try again. Tiny tots try, try again until they succeed at so many things it should almost boggle our adult minds.

The universal practice of testing in the public schools produces countless failed attempts at succeeding. These unnatural failures diminish the natural desire to succeed in many children. Testing is a form of failure, a student-defeating behavior most teachers know not how to otherwise employ. Testing is part and parcel of their brand of teaching.

When we as teachers, parent or otherwise, get the unnatural desire to test the children that are our students, we should at the very least turn those desires towards evaluation and forget the notion of testing. I have to say I don't truly evaluate my children's progress, as the word might connote, although I purport to do so. That's what I've told schooling authorities and I have also sold EVALUATION as one E of education in some of my seminars. No, I don't really evaluate. I guess I observe somewhat, but mostly, I just enjoy! Enjoying is my personal favorite E of education.

The most important E of education is EXAMPLE. If you forget everything but just one thing, remember example. If you spend time studying, reading, and having fun learning through play, your children will tend to be like you. Lead and your children will follow. Learn and your children will want to learn too. Read and they will want to know what you're reading about. Two more important E's of education are Encouragement and Excitement (choose encouragement over criticism and feel free to let your excitement for their progress show). This list could go on, but let me suffice with these last three E's of education: Example, Example, Example.

CONCLUSION

Before I quite conclude, I'd like to apologize for causing any defensive, negative or guilty feelings in any parents who read my works. I'm trying to share a learning alternative that is very real, feasible, easy and natural while seeming so foreign to so many.

I realize that not everyone can take advantage of the wonderful educational choices I've found at home, for various reasons, but I hope those people can glean something useful to them from within these covers. Whether or not parents can stay home with their children part or full time, they can foster natural home schooling *when* they are home.

While I believe children who stay home to school have the greatest learning advantages, I know that even publicly schooled kids do better if their home fosters a healthy natural learning environment. Any good home can make up for a bad school.

Unfortunately, your challenges as a parent are greater in proportion to the time you share the parenting with others.

If people knew how easy and inexpensive natural learning in their homes can be, parents and children would flock to their homes in droves. This fact is one of the world's best kept secrets I'm trying to share. Natural home schooling is so easy, you'd have to spend a week at our house to comprehend.

My sincere advice is for every parent to simplify life enough to allow for as much natural home schooling as possible. Give up some *things* to give your children more of your time. With me at home with our kids, we have gone without many things our friends are enjoying while they both work to the tune of a double income, as they utilize the *free* child sitter that is the public school. I confess we still haven't started buying a house yet because the kids and their home schooling has been more of a priority than finding a way to muster up that elusive down payment.

Care for your children in shift work, between parents, extended family, friends or coworkers you trust, where and when you can. I've seen single and/or working parents do co-op home schools which have worked well for them, as baby-sitting swapping did when their kids were tots. Get creative and you'll find ways and means to ends that your children just may thank you for some day.

In conclusion, I'd like to clarify a few points. I know children (and ultimately all of us) can learn many things in many different ways. There are many methods and styles of teaching and learning that work more or less for more or less people. What works best or what is natural for each individual does vary. Tailor-made methods work best, because each person is unique.

Is there one ideal natural learning pattern? Perhaps. Who knows for sure? I don't. But, I do tend to believe in something natural which is along the lines of how children learn to walk and talk: at their own pace, self-directed, with parental guidance, including ensuing enthusiasm and exultant cheering.

I am not against all structured teaching: sometimes it seems to work its way into the learning process naturally and sometimes kids even ask for such help.

I don't hate public schools. I certainly have nothing against public schooling kids and their parents. Some pro-public school people in my community protested against my first home schooling book (*HOME SCHOOLING: Answering Questions*), labeling it "hate literature" against the public schools (check it out and see if you agree).

I do believe that the state should get its big hands and feet out of the school business, as it has heretofore done. Privatising the whole schooling process, at first with vouchers, would help immensely. I do believe the school power should be in the hands of parents, and their children: the students; while state power should be given back into the hands of the people. Not people having power over other people, but over themselves.

As much as I believe in home schooling, naturally, I would never push and shove it upon anyone else; as I would never want public schooling, unnaturally, forced upon me and mine again.

Home schooling is what nature intended. Whether you believe in a Mother Nature or God the Father, it should be easy enough to see that there is a natural design for families on this earth. Whether you believe your rights as God given or just inherently human rights, you must believe in your right to raise your children yourself.

Through nature I have been given my children and it is right and natural that I give to them by raising, nurturing, teaching, guiding, providing for and protecting them. This is my right and my responsibility as a parent and I happily accept it. The right to grow and learn at home are my childrens'.

It saddens me greatly that so many millions of children for too many years have been raised in the name of public schooling without their parents' time and love. Taken from their parents at tender young ages they are forced into an unnatural institutional world before their time.

Home schooling is just a natural continuation of learning in the home: from birth, infancy and toddler-hood to childhood, puberty and young adulthood. Home is where the heart is, where love abounds (at least it should and if it does not, it is only a house, because love makes a house a home).

Natural learning happens as a whole, not really in separated, unnatural parts. Learning is a natural holistic integral part of home and family. Home is where the most important learning can and does happen. Home is the best place to learn, naturally. Home schooling is as simple as one, two, three: loving, living and learning, together at Home Sweet Home, Naturally!

NOTED HOME SCHOOLERS:

Adams, Ansel (Photographer)
Adams, John Quincy (6th President U.S.)
Adenauer, Konrad, (Statesman)
Andersen, Hans Christian (Author)
Bell, Alexander Graham (Scientist, Inventor)
Buck, Pearl (Writer)
Burroughs, John (Naturalist, Essayist)
Carnegie, Andrew (Industrialist, Manufacturer, Philanthropist)
Carver, George Washington (Scientist)
Chaplin, Charles (Actor, Director, Mime, Producer)
Christie, Agatha (Novelist)
Churchill, Winston (Author, PM England, Statesman)
Clark, George Rogers (Explorer, Soldier)
Colfax, Grant, Drew and Reed (Harvard Scholars)
Coward, Noel (Actor, Author, Composer, Playwright)
Curie, Pierre (Scientist)
Dickens, Charles (Novelist)
Edison, Thomas (Inventor)
Franklin, Benjamin (Author, Diplomat, Inventor, Scientist, Statesman)
Harrison, William Henry (9th President U.S.)
Harte, Bret (Writer)
Henry, Patrick (Statesman)
Jackson, Stonewall (General)
Lee, Robert E. (General)
Lewis, C. S. (Essayist, Novelist)
Lincoln, Abraham (16th President U.S.)
MacArthur, Douglas (General)
Madison, James (4th President U.S.)
McCormick, Cyrus (Inventor)
McKinney, Tamara, (World Cup Skier)
Mead, Margaret (Anthropologist)
Monet, Claude (Artist/Painter)
O'Connor, Sandra (Jurist)
Patton, George (General)
Penn, William (Statesman)
Pheonix, River (Actor)

Roosevelt, Franklin Delano (32nd President U.S.)
Schweitzer, Albert (Doctor, Musician, Writer)
Shaw, George Bernard (Dramatist, Novelist)
Smith, Joseph (Mormon Church Founder)
Terman, Fred (Educator)
Vandiver, Frank (Educator)
da Vinci, Leonardo (Artist/Painter, Architect, Engineer, Mathematician, Musician, Scientist, Sculptor)
Washington, George (1st President U.S.)
Wilson, Woodrow (28th President U.S.)
Wright, Frank Lloyd (Architect)
Wright, Orville and Wilbur (Inventors)
Wyeth, Andrew and Jamie (Artist/Painters)

(This list is only the beginning of the list of home schoolers who have made a mark on the world as leaders on their chosen paths. There are many more from the past, in the present and future who could be added to this list.)

SUGGESTED READING LIST:

And the Children Played by Patricia Joudry (Montreal: Plattsburgh NY: Tundra Books, 1975)

Don't Teach, Let Me Learn by Nina Crosby (Buffalo NY: D.O.K. Publishers, 1980)

Home Schooling: Answering Questions by Kerri Bennett Williamson (Springfield IL: Charles C Thomas, 1989)

Home Schooling for Excellence by David and Micki Colfax (Mountain House Press, 1987)

Home Spun Schools by Raymond and Dorothy Moore (Waco TX: Word Books, 1982)

School's Out: Hyperlearning, the new technology, and the end of education by Lewis J. Perelman (New York: William Morrow, 1992)

Teach Your Own by John Holt (New York: Delacorte Press/Seymour Lawrence, 1981)

The Home School Challenge by Donn Reed (Glassville NB: Brook Farm Books, 1985)

The Moore Report International, a newsletter put out by The Moore Foundation (founded by Raymond and Dorothy Moore) (P.O. Box 1, Camas WA 98607)

Growing Without Schooling, a newsletter founded by the late John Holt (729 Boylston St., Boston MA, 02116)

Education Otherwise, a newsletter in Britain (25 Common Lane, Hemmingford Abbots, Cambridgeshire, PE18 9AN)